To Julia,
with lo
Rachael x.

CONFIDENT AS F*CK

9 Bold Moves for Midlife Women to Rewrite the Rules, Ditch Imposter Syndrome and Finally Take Centre Stage

Rachael Lawrence

Confident As F*ck
9 Bold Moves for Midlife Women to Rewrite the Rules, Ditch Imposter Syndrome and Finally Take Centre Stage

ISBN: 9781919315003 Paperback

Published by: Inspired By Publishing

Acknowledgements

To all the women I've coached, mentored, walked beside and watched rise, you are the heartbeat of this book. With every single story you share with me, every DM, every tear on a Zoom call, every "I'm scared but I'm doing it anyway," you remind me why I do this work. You're not just clients, you're catalysts. You are the reason I never stop showing up.

To the woman holding this book in her hands right now – yes, you – thank you. Whether you're sitting in the quiet chaos of your life thinking, "Is this really it?" or standing on the edge of your next chapter, unsure if you're ready, thank you. Thank you for choosing yourself enough to turn these pages. Thank you for being brave enough to imagine a new version of you. Thank you for saying, "Not today, imposter syndrome," and walking forward anyway. I see you. I believe in you. And I wrote this book because I was you.

To the women who doubted me, dismissed me or tried to dim my light to make theirs shine brighter, thank you. You lit a fire you'll never be able to put out. The weak leaders I once tried to impress showed me exactly who I never want to be. Your whispers, silences and passive-aggressive moves were fuel. You didn't break me; you handed me the pen.

To the friends who ghosted me, outgrew me or wouldn't applaud when I won, thank you. Your absence cleared the space for something far greater. Every door that closed gave me the courage to build my own stage, one where women can rise without apology.

To my husband, thank you for standing shoulder to shoulder with me through this entire writing journey. You've given me space when I needed solitude, cheered me on when I doubted myself and held the line so I could pour everything I had into these pages. You've believed in this book (and in me) without question, and that faith has meant everything. To the family and friends who showed up in quiet ways – checking in, sending the occasional message or simply respecting the boundaries I needed to see this through – your presence, however small or steady, didn't go unnoticed. You reminded me that support doesn't always have to be loud to matter.

To every woman who ever felt she was too much, too little or too late, this is your permission slip. And your proof.

You can rewrite everything.

And finally, to my past self, on the kitchen floor, broken, a fucking mess, unsure how to move forward. You got up. You kept going. You dared to believe there was more.

You were right.

With fierce gratitude and endless love,

Rachael

Contents

Introduction

Midlife can be powerful.

It's the moment in life when you realise you've lived enough to know exactly who you are and you're no longer willing to shrink to fit.

You've survived heartbreak. Bounced back from burnout. Reinvented yourself more times than you can count. You've held everything together when the world around you was falling apart.

But now? Something's shifting.

It starts as a whisper, a subtle poke in the ribs, a quiet voice that says, "I want more than this."

No one warns you that right alongside that desire comes a midlife identity crisis that drops into your Google Calendar like an inconvenient unscheduled meeting.

Maybe you've spent the past few years being the capable one, the strong one, the fixer, the one who just gets on with it. But lately, something feels off. You're in meetings, nodding along, wondering if someone's going to realise you feel totally unqualified. You're putting on makeup for yet another Zoom call and can barely recognise the face staring back. You're hitting milestones on paper but still asking yourself, "Why don't I feel confident? Why do I still doubt myself?"

You've done the work. You've read the books, journaled your heart out, pinned your vision board with military precision and yet something still feels...misaligned.

The sneaky voice of self-doubt is whispering: "You're not ready," "You're not good enough," "It's too late to start over now." It's exhausting. Frustrating. Infuriating.

But here's what I want you to know: It doesn't have to stay that way. Midlife can be magical. Not in the filtered, perfect-life kind of way, but in the soul-deep, no-more-bullshit, I-know-who-I-am kind of way.

It's the season where you stop editing yourself to fit into rooms that never saw your brilliance. Where you stop whispering and start owning your worth – fully, loudly and without apology.

It's also the time in your life when you crave more: More meaning. More confidence. More you.

Maybe you love parts of your life.

You've built something solid: a business, a family, a career. You're the go-to woman in your workplace. You've started saying no to things that drain you. You've found sparks of joy in new hobbies or a friendship that feels like sunshine. But still, something tugs at your sleeve. You know you're not showing up fully. Not yet. There's a version of you you've been quietly editing for years. Softening your edges. Shrinking your voice. Playing a smaller game than you want to.

And you're done with that now, aren't you?

That's why I wrote this book.

There's a moment in every woman's life when she realises she's been slowly shrinking herself to meet expectations, allowing fear and other people's opinions to shape her choices, dim her light and quietly convince her that she's either too much or not enough. And yet she still aches to find the courage to hit publish on the real version of herself.

I believe that time, for you, is right now.

If you're reading this, you're likely standing in a beautiful life you feel you've outgrown. Maybe you're sitting at your desk wondering, "Is it too late to pivot in my career?" Hiding in the office bathroom, dreading the meeting you're about to lead, whispering, "I'm not qualified for this." Curled up on the sofa, scrolling socials, watching everyone else succeed, thinking, "Why can't that be me?"

Does any of that hit?

I know exactly where you are. Not long ago, I was there too. Stuck at a crossroads. Torn between thinking it's too late and knowing, deep down, there's so much more I'm meant to be, do and feel.

I've been the one sobbing in the bathroom, too scared to show up. The one who worked on a book for a year but couldn't hit publish. The one too foggy with overwhelm to remember why the hell I started a podcast in the first place.

But I learned how to unravel all of it, how to move from doubt to clarity, from exhaustion to confidence, from self-editing to self-expression. And once I figured it out, I knew I could help other women do it too.

That's why this book isn't just a pep talk; it's your permission slip. To silence that voice, reclaim your confidence and finally claim the authentic success you deeply deserve.

Let's call imposter syndrome what it really is. It's a sneaky, deeply rooted belief system that undermines everything you've worked for. It tells you you're one mistake away from being found out. It keeps you busy, burnt out and playing small, hiding behind perfectionism and procrastination. It convinces you you're not ready. Not worthy. Not enough. Despite all the evidence that says otherwise.

It's especially vicious to midlife women, the ones who've spent decades building families, careers, businesses and yet still question their value.

And it's not just internal. Left unchecked, it chips away at your health, your joy, your energy, your relationships and your potential. But it doesn't have to win. Because midlife isn't a crisis, it's a f*cking comeback. The narrative might try to tell you your best years have passed, that you should've figured it all out by now. I'm here to call complete bullshit on that. Midlife is your neon sign. Not a warning that time is running out, but a blinding signal that it's time to reinvent, reclaim and redefine what success looks like for you.

If you ignore the call, you risk staying stuck in careers that drain you, relationships that diminish and friendships that no longer fit. You risk living your most powerful years in someone else's story. And honestly? We're not doing that anymore.

Because imagine the alternative.

Imagine silencing your inner critic. Stepping into your full power. Making bold, aligned decisions from a place of self-trust. Negotiating your worth. Leading with confidence. Living the life you've always felt was just out of reach. Imagine holding your head high and saying, "Through all the shit, I still got what I wanted."

I didn't write this book from a pedestal. I wrote it from the messy trenches of real life, fuelled by one particular February morning in 2023.

I was on my kitchen floor, crying into my dressing gown, holding a cup of Earl Grey that had gone cold. The world outside was "bouncing back." Everyone else seemed to have a plan. I felt like I'd been chewed up by the past few years and spat out into a life I didn't recognise. Solo motherhood. A coaching business I couldn't find the energy to lead. A property business still limping post-pandemic. Burnout in full force. My podcast mic was gathering dust. My writing felt forced. My creativity was gone. My confidence, the thing that used to carry me, had vanished into the fog. I wasn't just questioning my career; I was questioning everything. Was I still a coach? Was I still relevant? Had I missed the boat? Was I too late to start over?

I'd been carrying so much for so long, showing up for everyone but myself, and I was done pretending I had a plan. In that moment, I heard a whisper. The same whisper I know you've heard, too: "You're not done. You're changing." That wasn't a breakdown. It was a breakthrough.

Midlife wasn't my crisis. It was my wake-up call. My rise-up call. I decided I wasn't available for self-doubt, imposter syndrome or living in survival mode anymore. I closed the door on old stories. I chose to do the damn work and figure out what I needed to feel like me again. And I did. That's why I'm here. Not as an expert on a throne, but as a woman who's walked through the fire, rebuilt her confidence, reclaimed her voice and is now handing you the match.

This isn't just another self-help book destined to gather dust on your nightstand. This is your no-BS, empathy-driven, action-focused guide to:

- Defining success on your own terms
- Quieting imposter syndrome
- Cultivating unstoppable confidence
- Making brave, aligned decisions
- Creating a life that feels like home

Each chapter will support your transformation from the inside out, starting with your mindset and rippling through your relationships, career and self-worth.

Here's what I know for sure.

The life you secretly dream about? It's not too late. It's not just a possibility; it's already waiting.

The confidence, clarity and courage you crave aren't reserved for "lucky" women. They're available to you the moment you say: "I'm done hiding."

So if you're tired of editing yourself for everyone else, tired of shrinking to make others comfortable, tired of waiting for permission to be fully you, then welcome. This is your Confident As F*ck moment.

Your midlife isn't a crisis. It's your boldest, bravest chapter yet. Your dreams matter. Your voice matters. You matter.

Let's do this because your life is ready.

And now, so are you.

Rachael xoxo
(Your new fan)

1
Own Your Power

How would it feel to step fully into your self-worth, capabilities and desires without self-doubt, fear and imposter syndrome keeping you stuck?

Imagine finally embracing your true, authentic self and permitting yourself to go after everything you want. Picture how it will feel when you own your confidence and achieve every single item pinned on your vision board. When you walk into that networking event, ready to have bold conversations, connecting as if you've done it for years because you know exactly what you bring to the table. When you walk into your yearly review and ask for that pay rise, because you deserve it. When you pitch for the business and know, without hesitation, that you can solve your clients' problems.

I see you.

I know that, for too long, you've navigated around that nagging imposter syndrome instead of confronting it head-on. You've shrunk yourself in meetings, hesitated to speak up, avoided opportunities and let self-doubt keep you stuck. You've procrastinated, felt overwhelmed and questioned where you're going in your business or career. You've been caught in the comparison trap, doom-scrolling on social media, desperate to figure out what you should be doing to achieve the success you see in other women.

I know this because I've been there too. And here's what I know to be the truth:

> Playing small is costing you, in income, impact and fulfilment.
>
> Confidence will not magically appear one day. You have to claim it.
>
> The women you follow on social media? They're most likely not showing you the blood, sweat and tears it took to get where they are.

If you want to build an authentic brand and business, lead with authority or claim the next rung on the career ladder, you must learn how to step through imposter syndrome, out of your comfort zone and into your courageous zone.

I know these truths are terrifying. Facing these fears head-on feels like too much. But that's why I'm here. I'm going to show you exactly how to handle it all.

And you're not alone. There are millions of women just like you (myself included).

What you're experiencing has a name; it's called imposter syndrome. And it's more common than you think.

At its core, imposter syndrome is the persistent belief that you're not as capable, intelligent or talented as people think you are. It's the voice in your head whispering, "Who do you think you are?" even after you've achieved something brilliant. It's the feeling that at any moment, someone's going to "find you out" and realise you're not good enough. It shows up as perfectionism, procrastination, people-pleasing and constantly second-guessing yourself, even when you know what you're doing.

As if that wasn't enough, imposter syndrome doesn't go away the more you achieve. In fact, the more successful you become, the higher the stakes and the brighter the spotlight, the louder it can get.

This isn't just a feeling. Research shows that imposter syndrome is far more common than most women realise. A KPMG study found that up to 75% of female executives experience imposter syndrome at some point in their careers, especially during moments of career transition.[1] That means three out of four women in senior roles are quietly battling the same doubts about whether they're "enough."

The struggle isn't just internal. A survey of 2,000 women revealed that by around age 36, many begin to feel "invisible" in work and social situations, with 44% reporting they were being overlooked in their workplaces and social settings.[2] The timing is telling: Just as women are stepping into their peak years of experience, they're often made to feel as though they no longer matter.

On top of this, research continues to show that women are less likely than men to self-promote, negotiate salaries or take credit for their achievements, all behaviours that contribute to the gender pay gap and chronic under-recognition.[3] It's not that women don't have the capability; it's that cultural and structural barriers make it harder for them to own and communicate their worth.

And the impact runs deep. Imposter syndrome has been directly linked to perfectionism, procrastination and self-sabotage, all of which can spiral into burnout and missed opportunities.[4,5] The data tells a powerful story: Imposter syndrome isn't just an occasional wobble; it's a patterned, predictable challenge that holds too many brilliant women back.

These are not just numbers or random statistics. These are the real-life patterns I see in brilliant, capable women every day, maybe even in you.

Maybe you're the highly skilled businesswoman who undercharges because you doubt your expertise.

Maybe you're the corporate leader who stays silent in meetings for fear of sounding "not smart enough."

Maybe you're the midlife entrepreneur who avoids being visible online because you dread judgment from friends and family.

Maybe you're the creative who hasn't launched her dream project because you're convinced you need one more qualification to be "ready."

Maybe you're the woman in leadership who constantly second-guesses herself and apologises for decisions she had every right to make.

Or maybe you're the experienced coach who hesitates to market her brilliance because, deep down, she still feels like a fraud.

If any of this feels familiar, let me tell you now: You are not alone. And you are not broken. This is what imposter syndrome looks like. But it's not who you are. And it's not where your story ends.

If you don't face your fears and self-doubt head-on, you'll stay in limbo. You'll want more for yourself, but never fully step into it. You'll stay invisible, missing opportunities for professional growth. You'll stay underpaid and undervalued because you won't assert your worth. You'll remain stuck in the self-perpetuating cycles of procrastination, perfectionism and hesitation.

How do I know this? Because I've lived it. And because imposter syndrome is a cycle. Until you unravel the limiting beliefs and behaviours keeping you stuck, you will remain paralysed, unable to bring your vision to life.

And here's what happens when you finally decide to face it: You stop second-guessing your brilliance and start showing up with clarity and confidence. You begin to speak up in rooms where you once shrank back. You stop waiting to feel "ready" and start claiming opportunities with both hands. The more you own your expertise, the more aligned success finds you, whether that's new clients, leadership roles, recognition at work or finally being paid what you know you're worth. You're no longer sitting on the sidelines of your own life. You're actively shaping it, one bold step at a time.

Here's one thing I've come to realise in the 20 years of doing this work: Confidence doesn't just magically appear one day, tapping you on the shoulder pads of your Chanel jacket and whispering in your ear to your imposter syndrome bestie. Confidence is something you have to claim for yourself.

And so this is where we start the magical work of healing your past wounds, the lies you tell yourself, the fears that keep you stuck where you are and the patterns of behaviour that you're sick to death of. It's time, my love, to do the damn work and cultivate that business and brand you dream of, pivot in your career, write the book you've longed to write, launch the podcast or simply start being so much kinder to yourself. Whatever it is you dream of, it's waiting for you on the other side of your imposter syndrome.

I know firsthand how paralysing imposter syndrome can be. I've had it since my teenage years and spent a large part of my life finding ways to avoid facing it. If there was a way out of something that scared me, I took it. I dodged difficult conversations, avoided pushing myself in my early career and turned down opportunities that felt too big for me to handle. Each time I let self-doubt win, I was left frustrated, overwhelmed and envious of the women who seemed to succeed effortlessly.

Then, in my mid-20s, I attended a Feel the Fear and Do It Anyway workshop. It was the first time I truly faced my limiting beliefs. I realised I had spent years cocooned in self-doubt, convincing myself that staying small was the safest option. But deep down, I knew I was lying to myself.

That workshop changed everything. I started working on my mindset, belief systems and fears. Over two years, I took small steps out of my comfort zone, pushing myself further each time. I delivered mental health training for large organisations, spoke on stage about my organ donation journey, started my life coaching practice, and many years later, even built a property business from scratch with zero funds (Yep, that happened! But that's another story for another day).

Fast forward to 2020. I had just celebrated my 40th birthday when the world went into lockdown. My property business took a massive hit, my tenants couldn't pay rent and my income disappeared overnight. My confidence plummeted. That old imposter syndrome crept back in, whispering, "See? I told you, you weren't good enough to become successful."

I had two choices: Give up or fight back. I chose the latter.

This time, though, I noticed something different. The mindset work I had done before hadn't disappeared. It was still there, like a well-worn muscle memory waiting to be activated. It was almost like my mind just needed a gentle reboot rather than a full reset. I still had those niggling doubts, those whispers of "maybe you're not good enough," but they didn't hold the same power over me. Instead of making me shrink and retreat, I recognised them for what they were. Just thoughts. Not facts and certainly not truths! And because I had already built the tools and strategies to navigate self-doubt, I knew exactly how to push through. I leaned into discomfort, stepped outside my comfort zone and did what needed to be done.

I rebuilt my coaching business, got clear on my vision, self-published *Reset Your Mind,* launched a podcast called *Blaze Your Own Trail,* rebranded myself and took bold steps forward. I remembered who the fuck I was. And now, I teach women like you how to do the same.

In this book, I'm going to take you through a coaching process that will help you uncover your self-limiting behaviours, ditch the imposter syndrome that's been running the show, and take bold, immediate action to break free.

So let's start with this. Grab yourself a beautiful journal, or use the pages in this book, light a candle, pour yourself a cup of something lovely and get ready to work out where you're playing small.

"No more playing small to keep the peace or fit the part.
The version of you that owns the room is ready,
and she's done waiting."

– Rachael Lawrence

Exercise

Step 1: Identify Where You're Playing Small

Ask yourself:

1. Where am I shrinking or holding back in my business/career?

____

____

2. When have I let self-doubt stop me from speaking up, showing up or claiming opportunities?

____

____

3. What excuses have I used to justify playing small?

4. After the above, write down three specific instances where you've downplayed your expertise, avoided stepping up or let fear lead the way.

5. How did getting all that down make you feel?

Step 2: Challenge the Inner Narrative

Most of the time, the stories we make up in our heads are simply not true. As midlife women, we've spent so long believing the false inner narrative and the "fake news" that we've become used to the burnout and exhaustion that results from tying ourselves in knots trying to figure it all out. We end up believing we're "not ready", "not experienced enough" and the classic, "not good enough!" But where's the evidence? And how do we stop this vicious cycle of beating ourselves up with negative self-talk?

It starts with reframing the story.

It's proven that speaking negatively to yourself can have a significant impact on physical and mental health. This causes us to experience heightened stress, anxiety and depression. As if that's not enough to send us over the edge, these emotions can then manifest in our physical bodies as digestive problems, sleep disturbances and hormonal imbalance – like we didn't already have enough of those in the first place.

It's time to take back control of that little voice in our head and to challenge it by starting with reframing the story.

Reframing the story looks like this:

INSTEAD OF		SAY THIS INSTEAD
"I always mess things up."	→	"I am learning and improving every day."
"I'm too old to start over."	→	"I have years of wisdom and experience that make me even more capable."
"I need to be perfect before I put myself out there."	→	"Taking action is what creates progress, not perfection."
"I'm just not a confident person."	→	"Confidence is something I build through experience and action."
"I don't have the qualifications others have."	→	"I have real-world experience and my perspective is valuable."
"I'm not good with money/business/technology."	→	"I am capable of learning anything with time and practice."
"If I try and fail, everyone will think I'm a fraud."	→	"Trying and failing is how every successful person grows."
"No one will take me seriously."	→	"I take myself seriously, and that's what matters."

INSTEAD OF		SAY THIS INSTEAD
"There are already so many people doing this."	→	"No one can do it exactly like me."
"I don't have the time."	→	"I get to choose what I prioritise, and I can make time for what matters."
"I'm not naturally talented at this."	→	"Every expert started as a beginner, and I can develop my skills."
"I don't deserve success."	→	"I am worthy of success, happiness, and fulfilment just as much as anyone else."

Step 3: Take One Bold Action Right Now

It's time to come out from underneath your invisibility cloak. You know what I'm talking about: the comfort blanket you wrap around yourself when you want to make the bold move, take the steps you need to take and put yourself first. The only way to do that is to stop playing small and take up space! No overthinking or procrastinating. Just one courageous move today.

Pick one:

- Speak up in a meeting or networking event
- Pitch yourself for an opportunity (a collaboration, podcast, article or leadership role)
- Increase your prices or finally tell a client: "These are my rates."
- Post online about your expertise instead of waiting for the "perfect" moment

Remember: Small daily acts of boldness create lifelong confidence.

Practice

For the next seven days, I want you to take one daily action that stretches your confidence muscle. Each time you feel hesitation creeping in, ask yourself, "What would the most powerful version of me do right now?"

In September 2010, I worked with a client named Conrad who didn't believe this exercise would work. His negative thinking was *loud* and left him feeling frustrated, embarrassed and lonely. He carried a lot of self-doubt and wasn't convinced this particular exercise would help him. So I challenged him to try it for a week and see what happened.

During this week, he visualised an actual monkey on his shoulder whispering in his ear every time he was stepping out of his comfort zone. He would physically flick his shoulder to shove the monkey off his back and tell him to fuck off. After a week of becoming aware every single time he heard the negative monkey voice and physically flicking him off, he found that he felt stronger in his body and more empowered to make the bold, scary moves.

It didn't surprise me that within three months of our session, he had gained a promotion at work that came with a significant pay rise, found the courage to start recording his guitar music and play in front of audiences. He had even pushed himself further by dating again, something he had previously written off.

Now I know Conrad wasn't a midlife woman! But his testimony is so powerful. When he first came to me, he was miserable, cynical and frankly, rude! He didn't believe any of this "stuff" was going to work. Eventually, he started to trust me and implemented what I was teaching. The transformation in him was remarkable and life-changing. I knew I had to find a place in this book to share his story because I think it's so relatable, regardless of your gender.

Final Thoughts

This is your line in the sand. You've spent enough time shrinking, second-guessing and waiting for some magical moment when you'll finally feel "ready."

That moment isn't coming. Confidence doesn't arrive like a perfectly wrapped parcel; it's something you choose, something you build, moment by messy, magnificent moment.

You already know you're meant for more; that's why you picked up this book. Now it's time to act like it. No, this isn't about suddenly becoming fearless; it's about deciding that your fear doesn't get to be the driver anymore. So stop trying to squeeze yourself into the version of you that plays small to make everyone else comfortable. Step up. Speak up and own your brilliance.

This is your time. I'll be right here beside you, cheering you on as you take up the space you were always meant to fill.

Confidence Cues

- Confidence isn't given, it's claimed, by you, for you.
- Playing small keeps you safe, but never satisfied.
- Imposter syndrome doesn't mean you're not capable; it means you're human.
- The first step to confidence is action, not perfection.
- You already have what it takes; you just have to believe it long enough to try.

"She remembered
who the hell
she was – and
everything
changed."

2
Your Inner Critic Is a Liar

What did she say to you this morning?

You know who I mean. That little bitch voice in your head. The one that woke up before you did, just so she could remind you that you're already behind before you've even had your coffee.

Was it something like this?

> "You can't wear that. Who do you think you are?"
>
> "You really think you're good enough for that job? Yeah, right."

"Might as well stay in bed; no one's going to take you seriously anyway."

"Don't post that, you look ridiculous!"

I mean, she really gets creative, doesn't she? If she had a LinkedIn page, her job title would be Chief Doubt Officer, Head of Self-Sabotage and Director of Talking Absolute Shit.

And yet, for some reason, we believe her.

We let this voice determine our choices, shrink our confidence, and keep us from taking the bold steps we *know* we need to take. But here's the truth: That voice? She's not you.

She's a liar. And today, we're shutting her up.

We've explored the ways you've been playing small, and now we dig deeper and uncover the why: Why you've been playing small. Why you've been doubting yourself. Why, even after years of experience, you still question whether you're good enough.

Because the answer almost always comes back to her – the inner critic.

So who is this "inner critic," and where does it come from?

The inner critic is the constant internal voice of fear, doubt and past conditioning. It's a repetitive voice that sits firmly in the subconscious, replaying all of your fears, your past failures and mistakes.

It thrives on all the old stories you tell yourself, it dismisses your achievements and blows your perceived failures out of proportion and keeps you in that constant cycle of perfectionism, hesitation and overthinking. *It's exhausting!!*

It's also a BIG, FAT LIAR.

Your inner critic is not a truth-teller; it's a fear-based survival technique.

We weren't born with it. It's a survival mechanism from when we were picking berries in our cave days. Back then, our brains were hardwired to detect danger. Our brains developed a self-monitoring system to keep us hyper-aware of danger, failure and rejection. Fast forward to today, and this same mechanism still exists. It's just evolved from warning us of actual danger into making us second-guess whether we're qualified enough to apply for a job, smart enough to build a business or worthy enough to take up space in the boardroom!

It isn't just evolution, it's our conditioning too. The people who influenced us throughout our lives – teachers, parents, religious leaders, ex-bosses and those mean girls from school – they've all left their echoes in our minds, reinforcing the doubts we carry with us today. The problem is, you've absorbed it all like a sponge and replayed their voices and scenarios so much that you believe every single thing they say. You probably haven't realised that up until now, the inner critic has been running the show because, as women, we've been taught to be realistic, cautious and humble. It's that voice that has been making your decisions for years.

Well, my love, I'm here to teach you this. That voice might sound like you, but it's not your truth. It was shaped by fear, by outdated rules, by the things other people said and did that left a mark.

But here's the good news. You don't have to believe it anymore. It's been running the show for far too long. And now? It's time to kick its ass.

A survey found that the average woman criticises herself about eight times per day, often starting before 9:30 AM. This adds up to more than 23,700 self-insults per year.[6] Is it any wonder our confidence feels too scary to step into?!

So let's get into what it says to you, without hanging on to the shame or guilt.

The Inner Critic's Greatest Hits (and Why They're Lies)

Here are some real-world, negative thought examples from women I've coached that demonstrate how the inner critic shows up for them on a regular basis! I'd like you to take a moment to read through each statement and see which ones you relate to by putting a cross or a tick next to each one.

- ☐ "You just got lucky."
- ☐ "Someone's going to find out you have no idea what you're doing."
- ☐ "You need another qualification before you can charge that much."

- ☐ "If you say no, they won't like you."
- ☐ "You're too much", and "You're not enough." (Because why not both, right?)
- ☐ "You're too old to start over."
- ☐ "What if you fail? Everyone will see."
- ☐ "Who do you think you are?"
- ☐ "You should be grateful for what you have. Don't be greedy."
- ☐ "You're not as good as [insert person you compare yourself to]."

If you find yourself relating to nearly all of these statements, that's okay. I want you to know that this is not failure. It's further proof that your inner critic has been running the show for far too long and it's time to show her the exit.

That little bitch, inner critic voice is the No. 1 reason you stay stuck. She is the reason that you can have all the skill, experience and talent in the world, but if her voice is louder than your logic, you'll never feel like you belong.

If you don't start calling out your inner critic for the liar she is, you'll stay stuck in those same frustrating loops, constantly second-guessing yourself, tiptoeing around risks and wasting precious time sitting on your potential instead of stepping into it. You'll play small, not because you aren't capable, but because you've been conditioned to doubt yourself.

When you do the work, when you learn to challenge those thoughts, interrupt them before they spiral and replace them with grounded truths, everything shifts. You begin to trust your own voice. You start to believe in your skills, your ideas, your worth. You move through imposter syndrome with more ease because you've trained your brain to spot the difference between fear and fact. And once you've done that? You're no longer waiting to be picked; you're backing yourself, every damn day.

My inner critic has always had a loud voice. Even now, after years of doing the deep work, she still pipes up from time to time.

The difference? She doesn't stop me anymore. In fact, she fuels me.

These days, when she starts talking crap, I recognise her instantly, roll my eyes and get on with what I'm doing. She's lost her power. But believe me, it wasn't always that way.

Let me take you back to 1996.

I had just landed a weekend job at an upscale shoe store on the high street. I thought it would be fun, surrounded by beautiful shoes and handbags, chatting with customers. Bliss, right?

Wrong.

One Saturday, my supervisor decided it was time for some "training." She asked me to pick a handbag to match a new pair of shoes. So off I went, excited to impress. I returned with what I thought was a brilliant match. She took one look at them, grabbed them out of my hands, and threw them across the shop floor before turning to me and calling me stupid.

I was humiliated. And it didn't stop there.

Every weekend, it was the same public put-downs, power plays and cutting remarks. Eventually, I plucked up the courage, grabbed the only expensive "uniform" pair of shoes I owned, and left.

I moved on to a full-time job in a health insurance company, hoping for a fresh start. Instead, I got a female boss who screamed at me daily in front of my colleagues in our open-plan office that my work "wasn't good enough." I stuck it out for two years, with it slowly chipping away at my self-esteem until I couldn't take it anymore.

Then came recruitment. I thought, "Surely this industry will be different."

But no. My manager, Yvonne (yes, I still remember her name), would grab the candidate profiles I had written, read them aloud in front of the office, and throw them across my desk multiple times a day until they met her impossible standards or she got bored with her daily game of humiliating me.

Over time, these repeated experiences created an inner critic that played on repeat certain beliefs I carried with me for years: I wasn't good enough. I wasn't smart enough. I couldn't get anything right.

The message landed so deeply in my nervous system that eventually, I thought: "Maybe I'm just not cut out for this."

And so, I decided employment wasn't for me. I chose self-employment, my own business, my own rules and no female leader to humiliate me.

But, unfortunately, that didn't silence the voice. The inner critic had made herself at home. She still showed up every single time I attempted something new: "Who do you think you are?" "You'll never be successful." "You're not clever enough to make this work." "Everyone thinks you're a joke."

That voice stayed with me for years, until I found self-help, therapy, coaching and eventually, my purpose.

Through years of inner work, I rewired the beliefs that had been instilled in me by other weak women in leadership, women who were never taught how to lead with compassion, who had never done their own inner work, and who, sadly, passed on their pain.

The work was hard. It hurt me to face up to the humiliating experiences and relive them. But it was also powerful.

And it's what led me here, to coaching women like you, women with ambition and brilliance who are haunted by a voice that isn't even theirs.

I became the mentor I desperately needed when I was that 18-year-old girl in the shoe shop, having beautiful handbags thrown in my face and being called stupid.

Many years later, I now understand those experiences weren't punishments; they were preparation. Preparation for something so wonderful and empowering. They shaped me into a strong, confident, successful woman. A leader. A truth-teller. A coach with vision and purpose and a powerful message.

And I'm so proud that my journey has helped thousands of women transform their own.

I proved my inner bitch critic was a liar. And I want that for you too.

"Ok, Rachael, I hear you say all that, but how on earth do I shut her up?"

You start by finding ways to identify, dismantle and replace the negative self-talk with helpful, kind thoughts. Over time, this will help you develop a rock-solid belief about yourself that is positive, motivational and spurs you into taking the right actions to move you forward, instead of keeping you stuck in fear, perpetuation and your comfort zone.

This framework I'm about to share with you will encourage you to step into your confidence and reframe your outdated belief system. It will help you shut down the inner bitch voice.

It's time to grab your journal, or use these next pages to get it all down!

Exercise

Step 1: Recognise the Inner Critic's Lies

You can't fix what you don't notice. It's time to name the little bitch. By naming her and giving her a personality, she becomes easier to recognise and shut down. Here are some ideas to get you started:

- Panicky Pam
- Overthinker Olivia
- Dramatic Dana
- Worried Wendy
- Critical Chrissie
- Bossy Betty
- Rigid Rachael
- Mean Girl Molly

Earlier in this chapter, I gave you some real-world examples of the inner critic's greatest hits. What I want you to do now is to build on the ones you relate to and begin the process of challenging them. I'm hoping you've started to work out by now that most of what your inner critic says simply isn't true!

Write down five things your inner critic says to you the most often. Use the greatest hits earlier in this chapter if you need some inspiration. Label each one Fact or Fear.

1.

2.

3.

4.

5.

Step 2: Deconstruct the Inner Critic's Narrative

Taking the five things you've written above, I'd like you to replace the assumptions with facts. For example, if she says, "You're not experienced enough," ask yourself, "What proof do I have that I am?"

Instead of:

"I'm not smart enough," replace that thought with "I am resourceful and always learning."

"I don't belong here," becomes "I earned my place in this room."

"I don't have enough experience," becomes " I bring valuable skills and insight."

Make your own below:

____

____

____

____

____

Step 3: Develop an Inner Critic Shut-down Plan

Do you remember Conrad and how he developed a new habit of physically flicking the monkey off his back and telling it to fuck off every time he became aware of a negative thought? This conscious behaviour of flicking his shoulder enabled him to quickly recognise he was thinking negatively, acknowledge it and stop it before it spiralled, by telling it to "Fuck Off!" He then had to replace that negative thought with a new thought, one that was helpful, kind and moved him in the right direction of taking action, rather than keeping him stuck.

Pattern interrupts are useful tools when you are undoing the negativity you have repeatedly told yourself over and over. They can be as simple as flicking your shoulder and saying "Not now" out loud or snapping a band on your wrist for a short, sharp, instant reminder.

What we need to do now is help you develop a pattern interrupt that will quickly and easily help you silence your inner critic and reframe your negative thoughts as soon as they pop up.

To do that, you can:

Create a go-to affirmation, e.g. " I choose confidence over fear" or " I'm a strong, confident woman." The latter is my absolute favourite and has saved me *many* times.

Use a pattern interrupt, e.g. say "not today" out loud when a negative thought comes up, or imagine physically flicking the voice off your shoulder like Conrad did.

Have a "power file" of compliments, achievements and wins to counteract any doubt you feel.

Surround yourself with your cheerleading squad: the truth tellers, the mentors, friends and colleagues who remind you of who the fuck you are!

I want you to know that this is a practice and habit that develops over time. Your inner critic will still occasionally pop right up out of the blue to test you when you least expect it, but by doing this exercise regularly, you will gain the tools to put her firmly back in her box!

The more you do this, the more it will become second nature. Over time, your inner critic will pipe down. Remember, we are learning new habits to dismantle old thought patterns so you can step into confidence and shut her up anytime you need to. We are not trying to overcome or step out of imposter syndrome overnight.

Practice

For the next seven days, I'd like you to practise these new habits every time your inner critic shows up. I want you to immediately replace the negative thoughts with empowering, positive, motivational truths, develop a pattern interrupt that works for you and give yourself credit each time you do.

This new practice, my love, is how you start to build an authentic identity based on truth, not fear. Each time you challenge her, you're creating the space for your voice to be the loudest one in the room. This is how we start to show up for ourselves and step into our confidence.

This is exactly what happened to Lucy. In July 2002, Lucy came to me as a midlife professional who had left her career in HR to start her own coaching practice. On paper, she was brilliant: two decades of experience, glowing testimonials, a heart of gold. But she couldn't bring herself to charge for her services. She'd whisper her rates at the end of a call, then immediately discount them or add on extra hours for free.

Her inner critic had her wrapped up in a cycle of shame and guilt.

> "You don't have a formal coaching qualification, so you can't charge properly."
>
> "They're going to realise you're not as good as you seem."
>
> "If you ask for money, they'll think you're greedy."

Sound familiar?

In our sessions, we dug deep. She traced that voice back to her school years, teachers who praised her quietly but never publicly, a mother who told her not to "brag," and former bosses who always gave her the "nice girl" feedback but passed her over for promotion. Lucy remembered the feelings of not being good enough, the shame she felt for wanting recognition and the anger connected to those situations. Using everything she learned in our sessions, she managed over time to choose truth over the inner bitch voice, the stories she had been telling herself, and unravelled the lies.

Together, we worked on rewriting her internal script and built a "proof portfolio," a collection of success stories, kind messages from clients and real, measurable impact. She began to recognise that her value didn't come from recognition or a certificate; it came from the life-changing transformation and the impact she offered.

Within six weeks, Lucy raised her rates and said them out loud with confidence. Within three months, she had a waitlist. And by the end of our time together, she told me, "I used to think I had to prove myself to be taken seriously. Now, I just show up with intention, and that's enough."

She finally learned how to shut down her inner critic, and it changed everything.

Final Thoughts

Your inner critic isn't a truth-teller; she's just a noisy inner child, built on fear, old wounds and stories that no longer serve you. That voice in your head? She's not you. She's a mash-up of past experiences, other people's insecurities and outdated survival mechanisms that once tried to protect you, but now just hold you back.

You don't need to earn your way into confidence; you get to own it. From this point forward, your voice gets to lead the way. Confidence doesn't mean your inner critic will never show up again; it means she no longer gets a front-row seat. Not anymore.

You're the woman in charge now, and every time you interrupt her bullshit, you're making space for a louder, wiser voice: Your own. Keep going. You're already rising.

Confidence Cues

- Your inner critic is loud, but she's not the truth.
- Not every thought deserves a spotlight or a seat at the table.
- Confidence begins when you stop letting fear run the show.
- You are not your past mistakes, you're your next bold move.
- Silencing the critic starts with speaking your truth louder.

"Confidence doesn't whisper – it walks in and takes up space."

3
Confidence Is a Habit

Let me tell you something that might just change your life: If you're waiting to feel confident before you take the leap, you'll be waiting forever.

Confidence is often misunderstood. It's not about being fearless, extroverted or the loudest voice in the room. It's not about having all the answers. Confidence is about having a deep level of self-trust. It's knowing that whatever happens, you can handle it. It's the steady inner belief that says, "I've got me."

So why do so many women struggle with it? Because we've been taught to doubt ourselves, conditioned to play nice, stay small and wait to be chosen. We've been rewarded for perfectionism, praised for people-pleasing and penalised for showing up boldly. We've been told that confidence is arrogance. And over time? We started believing our doubt was the truth.

Here's what I've come to know as the truth. Confidence is built in the doing; through small, courageous steps that prove to your nervous system, "I've got this." It's not something that magically arrives after reaching a goal or milestone in your life or career. And it most definitely isn't a one-time achievement or something reserved for a lucky few. It's a daily practice, one you get to choose, cultivate and work on every day.

It's not leading with alpha energy. It's not faking it until you make it. And it's most definitely not about being the loudest woman in the room. Confidence is a feeling. It's the deep, internal knowing that you can trust yourself, your voice, your decisions, your timing. It's the ability to back yourself, even when you feel your stomach churning with anxiety and don't feel 100% ready.

Like the woman who launches her business not because she woke up one morning miraculously confident and ready, but because she knows deep down that it's only through action she becomes ready. Or like the leader who, despite shaking like a leaf, starts speaking up in meetings. Or like the coach who uploads her first podcast even though her voice is trembling (me!).

Most women (myself included) don't wake up every morning with a perfectly aligned mindset and boundless energy. Usually they wake up, feel the fear, hear their inner bitch voice stir – and they show up anyway.

Like a muscle, confidence is something you work on. The more you build it up, the stronger it gets. It's a habit cultivated by taking consistent, aligned action. In fact, research published in the *European Journal of Social Psychology* suggests that on average, it takes 66 days to form a new habit.[7] Confidence isn't just a feeling; it's a behavioural practice you can train your brain to return to.

Today, my love, we are done waiting for confidence to announce its arrival. We're done playing small. We're done being invisible. Today, we learn how to step into our confidence, step by step, choice by choice, action by action.

This chapter is about helping you build confidence habits that quiet the noise of imposter syndrome and remind you that you're already more capable than you think.

So why does building authentic confidence matter so much?

Without confidence, you stay stuck in the waiting room of your own life, watching other women rise while you sit it out, telling yourself you're not ready.

Confidence isn't just important; it's essential if you want to build the life, business or leadership role you keep dreaming about. Think of it as fuel. Without it, you stay stuck in neutral, you overthink, procrastinate and play small. With an empty tank, you end up watching others race ahead. You stay in the trap of self-doubt and you never fully trust your voice, vision or value, whilst that authentic brand, business or promotion you desire so deeply gathers dust on the vision board.

What would happen if you decided to stop all that today? What would happen if you decided you're worthy of so much more? Worthy of feeling grounded, resilient and prepared for all the visibility, leadership and success that is available to you? What would happen if you decided it's time to take up space with intention and move forward with a concrete belief in yourself? I'll tell you what will happen. You will move faster, bolder and freer than ever before. You will cultivate more confidence than you ever thought possible for yourself. You will show up authentically, fully aligned and able to handle *anything* that is thrown at you. And I am ready and excited to show you how to step into that confidence – today.

Back in 2016, seven years after my divorce, I was stuck in what can only be described as a situationship. It was a long-distance "relationship" with a man who, to be fair, told me right from day one that he didn't want commitment. And what did I do? I decided to make it my personal mission to change his mind.

Because that's what women like us are taught, right?

That if we just love them harder, support them more, become smaller, quieter, sexier, thinner, then just maybe they'll finally choose us.

Except he didn't.

And truthfully? He was never going to.

I ignored all the red flags. I tolerated the emotional hot-and-cold, the long silences, the constant ambiguity. And the worst part? He used to call me fat. Repeatedly. Casually. Like it was a joke.

But it wasn't funny. It chipped away at me, at my confidence, my self-worth, my sense of what I deserved. I was showing up for him, shrinking myself to fit into his version of love, and I lost myself in the process.

Eventually, I hit breaking point. Not just because I couldn't take the emotional rollercoaster anymore (although that was exhausting!) but because I had a daughter watching. And I knew, deep in my soul, that I had to show her something better. I had to show her what no longer putting up with bullshit and not settling for anything that felt "off" looked like. So after seven years of driving the length of the country every other week, I ended it.

In the weeks that followed, I felt like I was crawling through broken glass. My confidence was gone. My sense of identity was lost. Thoughts of "How did I let myself be treated like that for so long?", "Who's going to want me now?", "He's taken my best years!" plagued me.

But one morning, somewhere between therapy, journaling and having a word with myself, I had a moment of clarity.

I realised I didn't need to show up for a man – I needed to show up for me. For what I wanted. For what I needed. For the woman I knew deep down I was ready to become.

And that's the day everything changed.

Fast forward to a last-minute girly holiday with my daughter to Greece. I was staying in a gorgeous hotel, newly single, emotionally hungover and still piecing myself back together. I remember standing in front of the mirror getting ready for breakfast and thinking, "Sod it."

I threw on a sheer dress, a pair of heels, and strutted down to the buffet, channelling full Bridget Jones meets Beyoncé energy. It felt wild and liberating, even. Maybe a little ridiculous. But it also felt authentic. It was me, unfiltered, free and finally not trying to perform or please anyone but myself.

And that's when he walked in.

Alistair. My now-husband.

He saw me, really saw me, because I was finally letting myself be seen. Not the version of me crafted to impress or win someone over. Just me. Raw, a bit patched together, radiant and real.

And here's what I know to be true, and what I want you to take from this, my love. Confidence doesn't come from someone choosing you. It comes from choosing yourself.

When I stopped pretending I was something I wasn't or chasing ideal outcomes, when I anchored back into my true self, my true identity, when I stopped waiting to feel "ready" and simply showed up as my damn self, that's when life met me at my new level of authenticity.

Everything changed for me when I made that decision.

That was the shift. I wasn't trying to prove anything anymore. I was finally choosing to believe that who I already was was enough.

Choosing yourself doesn't just apply to romantic relationships.

It means showing up fully for your audience, charging what you're worth, walking into a job interview knowing you damn well deserve the opportunity, pitching for a podcast with an enviable audience or choosing not to shrink in a meeting. Every situation is asking you to back yourself.

When you stop waiting for other people to pick you, approve you or praise you, everything changes.

Confidence isn't about chasing validation. It's about becoming so anchored in your own value and belief in yourself that you move forward, regardless of who claps.

Your Confidence Power Practice

Introducing the daily confidence code to silence self-doubt and take up space.

Think of this as your daily dose of boldness. A powerful little routine that helps you build unshakable self-trust, one Louboutin-filled step at a time. You don't need hours of journaling or a full moon ritual (unless you want one). This is about simple, doable, confidence-building actions that create real momentum in your life and business.

Here you will learn how to recognise the small wins, take micro risks, track your momentum and reinforce your identity. It all starts with figuring out your confidence-leaking habits.

Go ahead and grab your journal, or write in this space. It's time to do some inner work.

Exercise

Step 1: Spot the Confidence Leaks

Confidence isn't just about what you do; it's also about what's draining you.

People-pleasing, perfectionism, comparison and over-apologising. The list goes on! Feel free to add to it. These habits are sneaky little leaks in your confidence tank. We all have them, but we might not be consciously aware of them.

And so your first step in this daily practice is to become aware. Ask yourself: Where am I leaking confidence on a daily basis? Get it all down.

- People-pleasing
- Perfectionism
- Over-apologising
- Overworking to prove your worth
- Not celebrating your wins

- Comparing yourself to people online
- Avoiding opportunities
- Waiting to feel ready (My favourite!)

Where am I leaking confidence on a daily basis?

____

____

____

____

____

Become aware of them and start to track the patterns. Then choose differently.

Step 2: Build a Micro-Confidence Routine

Right before you slip out of bed in the morning, before you let the inner bitch voice take control, before your oat matcha latte, I want you to set your intention for the day.

I want you to ask yourself this: "What would a confident me do today?"

It could look like this:

- I'll send over the pitch I've been trying to write for weeks.
- I'll raise my prices.
- I'll go live or show up on social media.
- I'll send the damn email.
- I'll speak up in the meeting.
- I'll set a boundary with someone.
- I'll compliment myself in the mirror.
- I'll pitch myself for a podcast, panel or feature.
- I'll wear the outfit that makes me feel powerful.
- I'll share my story.
- I'll do the thing I've been waiting to feel ready for.

Confident me would:

____

____

____

At the end of the day, I want you to ask yourself:

What did I do today that fuelled my tank? (e.g. I read 10 minutes of this book, I did a mini workout, I meditated)

____

____

____

What did I do that built my confidence muscle? (e.g I set a boundary with someone, I went live on social media, I updated my LinkedIn Bio)

____

____

I've designed this daily practice to encourage you to make confidence a non-negotiable part of your day, like your skincare routine or checking your phone. So that it becomes a habit that you do religiously.

The Confidence Power Practice

Think of this as your daily dose of boldness; a simple, doable routine that builds unshakeable self-trust without the fluff.

Download your guided Confidence Power Practice at rachaellawrence.co.uk/book-bonuses using the password BOOKBONUSES.

It's totally free, so make sure you don't miss out. You can also scan the QR code to get access.

Book Bonuses

SCAN ME

Reinforce the Identity (Not Outcomes)

Now that you're starting to take bold, confidence-building action, it's time to lock it in by reinforcing the identity you're stepping into.

Remember, confidence grows when it's anchored to identity, not outcomes.

What does that actually mean?

It means your confidence shouldn't rely on whether someone claps for you today or whether everything goes perfectly. Confidence that lasts isn't built on external validation; it's built on who you decide you are, even when no one's watching.

You could smash a presentation and still feel insecure if your identity says, "I'm not really a leader."

You could get booked out with clients and still undercharge if your identity whispers, "I'm not experienced enough."

But when you start to shift your inner narrative from "I hope I did well enough today" to "This is who I am now. I'm the kind of woman who shows up, no matter what" – that's when confidence becomes second nature.

You don't have to wait to feel confident. You can simply decide: This is who I am now. And every action you take from that place reinforces the identity.

This is exactly what Emma did.

Let me tell you her story. In March 2024, Emma came to me in her late 40s, feeling completely lost. She'd just come out of a long-term relationship, her youngest child had left for university and she'd been made redundant after 15 years in the same company.

"I feel like I've been erased," she said in our first session. "I don't know who I am anymore, or what I'm even good at."

Underneath it all, what Emma was really struggling with was confidence – not the loud, outward kind, but the kind that says, "I trust myself to rebuild."

She had spent years defining herself by what she did for others: mum, wife, reliable team member, friend. But now, standing in front of a blank slate, her inner critic was screaming louder than ever: "You've left it too late." "No one wants to hear from a woman your age." "What if you try and fail? Everyone will see."

Emma didn't need to raise her prices. She needed to reclaim her voice. She needed to find herself again and build a life that felt like hers. So we got to work. Tiny steps. Every day.

I introduced her to what you now know as Your Confidence Power Practice.

Her first bold action? Going to a yoga class alone. Then she updated her LinkedIn profile with a new photo. Then, she attended a free creative writing workshop in her local town, something she'd dreamed of for years, but told herself she wasn't "qualified" for.

Each action terrified her. Each one lit her up. And slowly, the identity she'd buried all those years ago started to show up; not just a woman starting over, but a woman stepping into her next chapter. A woman who no longer needed permission to take up space. A woman who didn't wait to "feel ready" to rebuild.

Six months later, Emma sent me this:

> "I just did something I never thought I'd do, I booked a solo trip to Florence, just for me. I'm not running away. I'm running toward my life. And for the first time in years, I feel like I belong in it."

That, my love, is what happens when you stop waiting for confidence and start building it like your life depends on it.

Because in many ways, *it does.*

What I'd like you to do now is to feel into the energy of your life like your life depends on it. For the next seven days, practise taking one micro action that makes you feel proud. Track it, reflect on it and by the end of the week, you'll have formed a brand new neural pathway, one that says: "I can do hard things, and I don't need to wait for a permission slip or to feel ready."

Final Thoughts

Confidence isn't a destination; it's a decision you make daily, even on the messy days when you're having a bad hair day and your inner critic's doing the latest TikTok dance in your head.

It's not something you wait around for, like a delivery that never shows; it's something you build with small, intentional choices, day after day. Confidence is a habit, not a happy accident. It's the identity you step into when no one's clapping yet, but you show up anyway. Whether you're walking into a pitch, standing up for yourself, or finally posting that reel, it's the act of choosing yourself in motion. You don't have to be perfect. You don't even have to feel ready. You just have to decide: "This is who I am now." And then prove it to yourself with action. That's how the shift happens. That's how you stop waiting and start rising.

Confidence Cues

- Confidence is a muscle. Work it daily, and it strengthens.
- You don't wait for confidence; you build it.
- Self-trust is the foundation of unstoppable confidence.
- It's not about being fearless; it's about taking action anyway.
- Aligned action > overthinking. Every. Time.

"Confidence is
the loudest
'no thanks'
you'll ever say to
self-doubt."

4
Stepping Into Your Confidence

You've spent too long playing the supporting character in your life. It's time to stop hovering in the background, shrinking and being invisible. Show up as the bold, main character in the movie that is *your* life, starting today.

You see, you *are* the main character in your life. Now, my love, it's time to start acting like it. I'm not talking about showing off, being loud, inauthentic or arrogant. Main character energy is none of those things; it doesn't require you to be something you're not.

Main character energy is all about showing up with your beautiful, feminine energy. It's about ownership, knowing your damn worth and having the kind of presence that turns heads. It's time to be seen and recognised as the beautiful, strong woman that, until now, has done a great job of remaining invisible.

This is where the work we have done in the last few chapters start to take shape. We've learned how to rebuild your confidence and silence your inner critic. Now the time has come to embody confidence like your life depends on it. Trust me, I know you're ready.

Here's what I've come to know in my 20 years of coaching women. Living your most confident midlife is your divine right. Your wisdom, all of your life experiences, have shaped every decision you've made up to this point. You don't need to hold on to standards and old versions of yourself that no longer serve you. The woman you are today deserves you showing up and taking your place.

Today, I want you to imagine you're channelling Samantha Jones' energy from *Sex and the City* (without the no-strings-attached sex – unless you want that, of course!). You deserve all the great things embodying main character energy brings.

We're changing things up, and not just in what you do as a career. I'm talking about how you speak. How you show up and how you carry yourself. Because here's another truth: The world responds to how you see yourself.

By the end of this chapter, you'll have forgotten who the supporting character – the old version of you – was. You won't even recognise her. You'll realise that when you step into main character energy, the whole world shifts and meets the newer, polished version of you right where you're meant to be: centre stage.

This chapter is your VIP invitation to stop playing small and start playing the lead.

Lipstick on, nails freshly manicured. Let's go.

I'm going to teach you how to step right into main character energy any time you want to.

So What Exactly Is Main Character Energy?

Main character energy is the unapologetic decision to show up fully for your own life, like it's the role you were born to play. It's choosing to stop hiding, stop waiting and start leading, with presence, power and a deep trust in who you already are.

It's walking into every room, every conversation and every opportunity knowing you belong there, because you've chosen to belong.

It's the difference between reacting to life and directing it, and that shift changes everything.

Now, I get it. This might feel off at first. We were taught not to show off, not to be too much, not to draw attention to ourselves. We've been conditioned to play small, to second-guess our voice, our style, our ambition. So stepping into this kind of energy might feel unnatural, even a little rebellious. But all the things you've been taught, to quiet down your brilliance, your power, your presence, are the very things that will move your life forward.

Main character energy isn't about pretending to be someone you're not. It's not about faking confidence or performing for approval. It's about remembering who you are at your core, and giving her the space to lead. This isn't the polished, perfect version of you. This is the grounded, powerful, self-led version, the one who doesn't need to prove anything to anyone. She just is. And she's finally ready to stop diluting herself.

When you begin to embody this energy, subtle shifts start to happen. You stop second-guessing the outfit that makes you feel powerful, and wear it without apology. You say yes to opportunities without knowing every detail, because you trust yourself to figure it out. You make decisions without justifying them to anyone else. You speak up in meetings, not to dominate, but because your voice belongs in the room. You show up online as yourself: clear, consistent, magnetic. You enter spaces you used to shrink in, and you leave them with new opportunities because your energy now reflects what you know: You belong.

When you don't step into this energy, you stay stuck in the same habits that keep you invisible. You keep playing small, feeling confused, frustrated and anxious that life isn't meeting you where you are, when really, you're still hiding under your invisibility cloak. You keep tweaking and overthinking. You wait for someone to pick you or promote you, all while quietly hiding in plain sight.

This chapter is your moment to stop waiting. Not for permission, not for perfection, not for someone else to validate you. Main character energy isn't a trend, it's a way of showing up for your life with intention, courage and self-respect. And the beauty of it? You don't have to feel ready to begin. You just have to decide you're no longer available for playing small.

Because confidence and main character energy aren't just habits. It's a way of being.

I learned this for myself for the first time back in 2010. I was sat in the Deloitte offices about to have a 1:1 meeting with John Binns MBE. I don't quite remember how the hell I managed to land this meeting. I honestly must've blacked out and typed the email without overthinking it, which, for me at that point, was a miracle in itself.

At the time, John Binns was well known in the corporate world for something far more courageous than his career success. He had publicly shared his experience of having a serious mental health breakdown while working as a senior partner at Deloitte. His honesty had sparked real change inside Deloitte, with the firm rolling out new mental health support strategies for its people. I was delivering a mental health course at the time, and I knew his story had the power to inspire organisations to support their employees better. That's why I needed that meeting, not for me, but for the lives and careers that I knew his experience could help save.

But there I was: 30 years old, preparing to meet a man who had been a partner at one of the most prestigious firms in the world. He'd experienced a mental health breakdown while climbing the career ladder at Deloitte, and I wanted, needed, to hear his story. I was building a mental health course, and I wanted to show people that not only is it possible to recover from mental ill health, it's likely. With the right support and honesty, you can come back stronger.

But I was shit scared.

Who was I to walk into Deloitte's glass palace of power suits and polished accents? Who was I to ask someone like him for a vulnerable, raw, honest interview? Imposter syndrome was *screaming*. And the anxiety? It had set up camp in my stomach for days.

Just the idea of travelling to London gave me palpitations, let alone navigating my way to those intimidating offices, walking in like I belonged. I had on a cheap suit that I prayed looked expensive and a pair of New Look heels that pinched with every step. I remember being sat on the wall outside quietly giving myself a good talking to, "Right,

Rachael. You will walk in like your suit is Chanel and your shoes are fucking Manolos."

So that's what I did.

I walked into Deloitte like I had done it a hundred times before. I sat in reception like I was meant to be there. And when I walked into that meeting room and shook John's hand, I channelled everything I had: my heart, my purpose, my clarity. I led with my feminine power and a handbag full of courage because I had fuck all else to fall back on.

I wasn't loud. I wasn't showy. But I was calm, clear and grounded in why I was there.

I needed this story. Not for me, but for all the people I was going to help.

And that's what did it. That's what unlocked the conversation.

John shared his experience, vulnerably, truthfully, generously. He trusted me enough to tell the story that would later inspire so many people in my workshops to believe that recovery is not just a possibility, it's a reality.

I walked out of that meeting room with something I hadn't expected. Yes, I had the interview. Yes, I had the content. But more than that, I had just discovered something about myself.

That day, in those cheap heels and a suit held together with hope, I had accessed something I didn't have a name for yet: Main character energy.

I had embodied confidence, even though I was terrified. I had led with intention, even though I felt out of place. I had claimed space in a room where my inner critic said I didn't belong. I held my own.

It wasn't about faking it. It was about rising to it.

And here's what I know now: That energy lives in all of us. Sometimes it takes being scared shitless and showing up anyway to find it. Sometimes it takes walking into a room you think you have no right to be in and realising you're the one who brings the value.

That was the day I stopped asking for permission to take up space. That was the day I stepped into my power, even if my feet were blistered.

That, my love, was the first time I met her, the main character version of me. And once you meet her, you never forget who you are again.

That meeting at Deloitte was the first time I consciously chose to show up as the main character in my life, even though everything in my body was screaming that I didn't belong there.

It wasn't confidence that got me through it. It was the embodiment of confidence. It was me deciding to show up anyway, as if I already belonged. I didn't wait to feel ready. I created the energy I needed by stepping into it.

That, my love, is what main character energy is all about.

It's not reserved for high-stakes meetings or "important" moments. It's a way of living. A way of choosing yourself in the everyday. A way of elevating your energy through small, consistent acts of self-leadership, even when the world feels chaotic or you wake up feeling like shit.

So what does it look like to live like the leading woman of your life?

Let me show you...

Romanticise the Ordinary

Romanticising the ordinary means elevating the everyday mundane into something more creative and magical, like serving up your green power juice in a champagne glass, wearing your favourite perfume to bed, ripping the tags off the dress that you've been saving for "date night" and wearing it out to lunch with your girls! The matching, sexy underwear gathering dust in your drawer? Wear it underneath your comfies on your next Zoom meeting. Your clothes are energy. And no, this isn't about being "put together" for others. This is about dressing in alignment with the version of you who knows she belongs. This new way of living is about elevating your everyday, mundane moments into little magic moments that lift your spirit.

Think: How can I elevate my everyday mundanity?

Honour the Frequency, Not the Mood

Now I understand you're not going to feel confident every single day. We're human after all! But on the days that feel meh, I don't want you to shrink back into the old version of you, or the "off" mood you've woken up in. I want you to keep honouring the frequency of the character you're learning to embody. Because the woman you are becoming isn't going to be perfect, but she is going to be consistent. She knows how to honour the frequency of her future self, no matter how she feels in the moment.

Main Character Energy isn't a mood. It's a frequency you return to, again and again. In moments of doubt, ask: What would the main character in my life choose right now? Then do that.

Speak in the Language of Power

Listen to yourself. Tune in to the language you are using. Speak in the language of power and drop the fluff. Drop the over-explaining. Drop the "sorry but..." and "just checking..." and "I was wondering if..."

Your voice is important, and the way you use it sets the tone for how people receive you.

Here's how to shift your language into power:

INSTEAD OF		SAY THIS INSTEAD
Sorry to bother you	→	I'd love your input on this

INSTEAD OF		SAY THIS INSTEAD
I'm just checking	→	I'm following up on our conversation
I think maybe we could try	→	I recommend we try
Does that make sense?	→	Let me know if you have any questions
Sorry, I just feel...	→	I believe or I know...

You don't have to dilute your language to be heard. When you remove the fluff and speak with clarity, people lean in and listen.

Make desires your roadmap, not your guilt.

Most women lead with what they should do. Main character energy leads with what she truly wants. Not in a reckless way, but in a deeply aligned way. When you start choosing what you desire, not what you're conditioned to accept, you reclaim your power.

Ask: What do I truly desire today, and what's one way I can honour it?

You don't need to wait to feel ready. You don't need more proof, more polish or more permission. The woman you've been waiting to become? She's already inside you. Main character energy isn't something you earn; it's something you choose. Every time you show up. Every time you speak up. Every time you decide not to shrink.

Because the world doesn't need another perfectly put-together woman. It needs you, real, radiant and unapologetically centre stage.

As a bonus for this chapter, I'm including my favourite, most impactful, "go to" affirmations that, when played on repeat in your mind, will help silence the inner bitch voice and help you walk into your next scary moment like you own the place.

Want to turn up the confidence on repeat?

I've created 20 powerful Main Character Affirmations to help you step into your next big moment like you already own the room.

Download your copy at rachaellawrence.co.uk/book-bonuses using the password BOOKBONUSES. It's totally free, so make sure you don't miss out. You can also scan the QR code to get access.

Book Bonuses

SCAN ME

Final Thoughts

Main character energy isn't about attention; it's about ownership. It's the energy that walks into a room and doesn't shrink to fit the vibe; it sets the tone. It's knowing who you are, trusting what you bring and standing in it without over-explaining or softening the edges.

You don't need to edit your personality, dim your brilliance or second-guess your presence. You get to walk with certainty, even when your knees are knocking.

That's real confidence. You don't become magnetic by doing what everyone else is doing; you do it by backing yourself fully and showing up in the boldness of who you already are.

This isn't about performance; it's about truth. And the truth is, you're done waiting for a nod from the outside world.

You're building a life that reflects who you really are. And that kind of self-belief? It's unstoppable.

Confidence Cues

- Main character energy is your birthright. Start acting like it.

- You belong in every room you walk into. Don't wait to be chosen.

- How you see yourself sets the tone for how others see you.

- Presence is louder than perfection.

- Confidence is magnetic when it's rooted in truth.

"When you own your story, no one gets to rewrite your power."

5
Progress Over Perfection

How many dreams have been postponed because you weren't "ready yet"? How many ideas have gathered dust because you were waiting for the right moment? How many versions of you have been kept small because you were trying to do it *perfectly*?

Let me guess.

You've got a beautiful planner with a to-do list longer than your arm. A million and one ideas swirling around in your head. A half-finished website, a ropy book outline, a podcast series planned but not recorded and at least three reels saved in your drafts folder.

But nothing's out there. Because it's "not ready yet." Am I right?

Now I know that, deep down, you know you're more than ready. But perfectionism keeps telling you: Wait a bit longer, get another opinion (probably from someone whose opinion shouldn't count), tweak that post, read one more book – reminding you over and over that you're *supposedly* not quite there yet.

This is what I call "the silent epidemic" that so many brilliant midlife women face.

Women who have a podcast idea...and still haven't recorded an episode. Have a book in their head but can't get past chapter one. Haven't updated their LinkedIn in years because "it's not ready." Postpone launching their offer because the sales page isn't "right." Hide behind Canva carousels and never show their face online. Google "how to start a business" and never hit go. Avoid dating apps because their profile isn't "good enough."

This isn't laziness. You definitely are not unmotivated. You are stuck in the exhausting, soul-sucking cycle of perfectionism and its sneaky best mate, procrastination.

So let's get a reality check here and break this down properly.

What is Perfectionism, Really?

Perfectionism isn't about striving for excellence or having high standards. Perfectionism has its roots firmly rooted in fear. You might fear being judged or not being good enough. You might have fears of failure or success, even. The problem is that fear can convince you that if you just make it perfect, you'll be safe. You'll be accepted. You'll be "worthy." But fear and perfectionism don't protect you; they paralyse you.

And as if that isn't bad enough, drum roll, please…in walks procrastination, dressed to the nines in a gorgeous Zimmerman gown. Now, I know you're not lazy, but when your standard is flawlessness, nothing ever feels good enough to even begin. So instead of making progress, you circle back over your plan, editing until you barely recognise what you started with, all the while convincing yourself you're polishing it to perfection. Maybe you scroll to distract yourself. Or maybe you stay "busy" endlessly reworking things instead of actually putting them into the world.

And the worst part? You probably beat yourself up for not doing enough, when really you've just been overthinking everything. You've worked eight hours straight – yet somehow feel like you've achieved absolutely nothing.

Here's what I want you to know.

Perfectionism and procrastination are not just best mates; they're symptoms of unhealed fear. And this fear, when left unchallenged, is what keeps powerful women like you small.

So if you're feeling stuck, overwhelmed, behind or frustrated by your own inaction, this chapter is for you. Because we're not meant to stay small, playing in this constant hot wash cycle. We're here to break it.

This chapter is your invitation to let go of the exhausting lie that everything needs to be perfect before you take action. It's time to release the impossible standards and remember that done is often far more powerful than perfect. Every time you choose progress over procrastination, you reclaim a little more of your confidence, your momentum and your life. In this chapter, you'll discover bold, feminine concepts that show you how to take messy, aligned, liberating action, even when it scares you. In doing so, you unlock the freedom and success that have been waiting for you all along.

We're rewriting the rules now. This isn't about ticking boxes. It's about learning how to move forward powerfully, especially when your inner bitch voice is begging you to wait. It's time to talk about the impossible standards we hold so dear to our hearts; the comparison, the competition, the completely messed-up version of ourselves that says, "I only do my best work when all the stars are in alignment, Mercury retrograde has finally fucked off and there isn't a full moon in sight!" It's time to admit that underneath your perfectly curated main character energy outfit, you're paddling like hell to stay afloat. And it's time to throw yourself the life jacket.

Admitting how debilitating your perfectionism fears are will blow the doors open to the life you're meant to be living. The version of you that's hiding behind "perfect" is not the version of you that finishes writing that book, launches the podcast or starts that business.

Your perfectionism isn't just holding you back from posting the reel or sending the pitch; it's keeping you stuck in a version of your life that feels safer than it does liberating.

And I get it. At this stage in life, you've already faced a lot: heartbreak, career curveballs, confidence knockdowns, motherhood, menopause, reinvention after reinvention. So it makes sense that you want to get it right this time. You want to be taken seriously. You don't want to waste time or energy on something that might flop.

Know this: The timing will never feel perfect. That's exactly why it's time to start.

I'm going to lay this on the line for you now. Midlife perfectionism is *painful*. It doesn't always look like colour-coded planners and beautifully laid-out Trello boards. Sometimes it looks like you "not having time" to do that thing you said mattered. Or waiting until the kids are settled…or until you've lost a stone…or until someone asks you to step up.

Perfectionism masks itself as productivity, but in reality, it's just fear dressed up in a shiny to-do list or a gorgeously curated outfit.

Let's talk about this moment in our lifetime. The pace of change is faster than ever. Women are starting businesses in their 40s and 50s, returning to education, going viral, publishing books and redefining leadership. But do you know what sets them apart? They are doing the scary thing: taking action before they feel "ready."

Not because they're braver than you. But because they've realised that perfection is a myth and that progress is the only way forward.

Right now, ask yourself this:

> How much longer am I going to wait for the timing to be perfect?
>
> How many opportunities am I going to pass by while I tweak my website font *again*? (I'm actually laughing out loud as I write this. I've rebranded my website *so many times*.)
>
> How many times am I going to watch someone with half my talent speak on that panel, land that client or launch that podcast because they were willing to move with imperfect courage?

This chapter is about giving you back your momentum.

Because without progress, your confidence can't grow. Without action, your boldest vision stays stuck in your head. And without release from perfectionism, your life remains a rough draft no one ever gets to read. I believe, in fact, *I know*, you deserve more than a life lived inside your drafts folder. And now is the time to claim it.

So what would happen if you chose progress instead?

You'd stop living in the someday and start creating a life that feels alive right now. That blog post you almost didn't publish? Imagine it landing in the hands of someone who's been waiting for your exact words. Imagine the impact that would have on them. That offer you launched before you felt ready? Picture it selling out and, more importantly, changing people's lives. That brave, shaky first podcast episode, recorded nervously at your kitchen table? Imagine it sparking a conversation that leads to your next big opportunity. The mastermind event that felt too hard to go to? You end up chatting to someone who can help connect you to someone big in your industry.

And do you know what's even better? Every time you take messy, imperfect action, you prove to yourself that you can handle it. That you can figure things out as you go. That you don't have to have it all perfectly lined up to be worthy of success, joy, connection or financial abundance.

You build confidence not by waiting for it to arrive but by watching yourself do the damn thing anyway.

So, love, ask yourself this: Am I willing to meet the version of me who lives beyond perfect? Because here's the truth: She's already out there, writing the pages, recording the podcast, speaking on that panel, cashing the payments, living the vibrant, fully expressed life you keep dreaming about.

All she's waiting for is you.

And this time, we're not keeping her waiting.

I wish I could tell you that I cracked the code on perfectionism years ago, that I saw the signs, snapped out of it, and never looked back.

But honestly? Perfectionism and procrastination kept me stuck for years.

Long after I'd trained as a coach, long after I'd delivered workshops that changed lives, I was still spinning in circles behind the scenes, editing, tweaking, avoiding, doubting. Not because I didn't care, but because I cared so much that the idea of doing it "wrong" made me freeze with fear.

Relaunching my coaching business? Terrifying. Writing my first book, *Reset Your Mind*?

It took over two years, not because I didn't know what to say, but because I was terrified I wasn't good enough to say it.

What if it didn't land? What if someone read it and thought, "Who does she think she is?" What if I published it, and no one cared? That fear didn't sound like "I'm scared," by the way. It sneakily disguised itself as "I just need to fine-tune this section." "I need to change the fonts again." "I need a better website." "I need to rename my podcast again."

And I did all of those things. I changed the colours and fonts on my website more times than I care to admit because I saw someone else on Instagram with a "better" brand. I changed my podcast name three times. I doubted every title, every post, every message. I kept polishing. Rewriting. Rearranging. It was absolutely exhausting!

But worse than that, do you know what all of that cost me?

Time.
Energy.

Opportunities.
And most of all, impact.

I missed out on helping women I knew I could serve, because I couldn't get out of my own damn way. My fear of not being "ready" meant I stayed invisible. What I told myself was that "refining" was really just me hiding. Even my friends would joke, "You still hiding underneath your invisibility cloak?"

But then, something happened. Something that slapped me straight in the face with truth.

I saw it in my daughter.

I noticed it for the first time in 2023, around exam time. She started rewriting her revision notes again and again because she made a tiny mistake. She'd redo her coursework from scratch, right up until the deadline, and hand it in, still thinking it wasn't good enough.

The problem was that her work was outstanding, but she couldn't see it. Because she'd absorbed that belief from someone. And that someone was me.

I realised I was modelling perfectionism. That I was teaching her, without saying a word, that unless something was flawless, it wasn't worthy. That done wasn't enough. That we wait, tweak and doubt until it feels perfect, whatever the hell that means.

And that broke me.

That was my turning point. I knew something had to change. For her. For me. For the women I'm here to serve.

So I stopped trying to be perfect and started taking action. And let me tell you, it wasn't easy.

It was hard to press publish on something I hadn't over-edited. It was hard to leave the font alone and let the message speak for itself (even in bloody Times New Roman). It was hard not to overthink every single thing I put out into the world.

But I felt the fear and did it anyway!

I made peace with "good enough." I launched before I was ready. I published *Reset Your Mind.* I relaunched my podcast for the last time. I got clearer on my message because I stopped hiding behind it.

And you know what happened?

The women showed up. The clients came. The feedback landed. The confidence grew.

Not because I perfected it. But because I finally released it. Was it perfect? Absolutely not!

Letting go of perfectionism didn't just help me make progress; it helped me get my power back. And that, my love, is exactly what I want for you.

Because the longer you wait for it to be perfect, the longer you wait to become the woman you already are.

So here I present to you, your mirror moment: What are you not doing because it's "not ready yet"? What masterpiece are you keeping hidden in your drafts folder?

Let's Get Real for a Minute

Okay, my love, this is the part where we pause, take a breath and get real with ourselves.

You've just read my story about how perfectionism and procrastination had me well and truly stuck. Maybe you saw yourself in it, maybe it made you laugh, maybe it made your stomach drop a bit. Either way, this is your moment. You're here reading this book for a reason. This book title jumped out at you and pulled at your gut feeling for a reason, or maybe your mate gave it to you.

Whatever it was that drew you to this book, please know that becoming aware of your procrastination and perfectionism is another step towards becoming *Confident As F*ck*!

So before we move into the how section of this chapter, I want to invite you to slow down and really reflect. Let's look at what perfectionism has been costing you. Let's name the fears that have been running the show. Let's hold up the mirror, not to judge yourself, but to see yourself clearly.

Remember, this isn't about shame. We're not beating ourselves up here. This is about you being honest with yourself, gaining clarity and finally feeling liberated.

You can't change what you're not willing to look at, and I promise you, nothing you uncover here is too messy or too much. I've been there, and I truly have seen it all. So grab your journal, give yourself 10 to 15 minutes to sit with these questions and answer these prompts with brutal honesty and the kind of self-love that says, "I am done standing in my own way."

Are you ready?

Journal Exercise

Where in your life or business are you waiting to feel "ready" before you take action? Be specific. Think about projects, decisions, conversations or ideas that you keep postponing.
•
•
•
•
•

What are you telling yourself will happen if you don't get it "just right"? What's the actual fear behind the perfection? Rejection? Embarrassment? Failure?
•   •   •   •   •

What is perfectionism really protecting you from? This one goes deep. Think about the safety of staying small vs. the risk of being seen.
•   •   •   •   •

Can you think of a time when you took action before you felt ready, and it worked out anyway? What did that teach you?

-
-
-
-
-

What's the cost of your perfectionism? Time, money, joy, creativity, visibility, impact? Name it. Bring it into the light.

-
-
-
-
-

If your daughter, best friend or a younger version of you was holding back because of fear, what would you tell her? Say it. Then say it to yourself.

-
-
-
-
-

What's one thing you could release today that would allow you to move forward, messy but proud? Your need for it to be perfect? The fantasy timeline? Someone else's opinion?

-
-
-
-
-

Reflection

Write one bold, beautiful affirmation you want to believe about taking action, even when it's imperfect.

Start with, "I give myself permission to…" and let it flow from there.

So… What Now?

By now, I'm really hoping you've realised something important. It's not your workload holding you back. It's not your lack of time, talent or ability. It's the internal pressure to get it right before you've even started.

So how do we let go of the hard stuff and move toward bold, aligned action – even when our brains are screaming, "This isn't ready yet!"

This next concept is something I wish I had figured out years ago instead of spending all that time, tweaking, doubting, reworking and hiding. It's designed to get you moving and shift you into your most feminine, authentic, new energy, your secret power that is dying to be let loose!

Because my love, it is time to get going, imperfectly, unapologetically, joyfully. Your dreams aren't waiting for perfection. They're waiting for you.

I want you to give this a bloody good go!

Good Enough Is Good Enough

Give yourself permission to create B+ work. Your 80% is someone else's lightbulb moment. That Canva post? Hit publish. That landing page? Email it. That Instagram reel? Upload it. The only person demanding perfection is you, and she needs a glass of wine and a nap.

Journaling prompt: Where am I holding back until it's "perfect"? What would happen if I just released it now?

The 24-Hour Rule

If it takes longer than 24 hours to finish something that doesn't need to be perfect, it's probably fear. Put a loving time cap on it. Treat it like a challenge: "Can I get this done and out in the world today?"

This builds self-trust fast. Action = evidence. You're training your brain to trust that you can move fast and be proud of your output.

Be a Bold Beginner

Being bad at something doesn't mean you're failing. It means you're learning. Adopt the energy of a bold beginner. Celebrate the fact you're in motion when others are still watching from the sidelines.

Journaling prompt: Where am I refusing to be a beginner because I'm scared of looking silly?

What could shift if I allowed myself to start messy?

____

____

____

Done Is a Feminist Act

Perfectionism is a tool of the patriarchy. (Yes, we're going there.) When women waste time editing, polishing and doubting, we stay quiet. We stay invisible.

We don't need another round of tweaks. We need more women hitting publish.

When you release something imperfect, you model bravery for every woman watching you. That's leadership.

Perfection Feeds the Inner Bitch Voice, Progress Starves It

Perfectionism gives your inner critic a megaphone. It thrives on your waiting. Progress silences it because taking authentic, feminine action builds your wonderful new Main Character Energy.

Try this: Every time you feel the pull to "just fix one more thing," pause and ask, "Is this fear, or is this finishing?"

Final Thoughts

You don't need to be perfect to be powerful; you just need to get going.

Perfectionism might be whispering that you're not ready yet, but waiting is costing you more than it's protecting you. The energy you've been pouring into tweaking, polishing and overthinking? That's fuel you could be using to change your life.

Confidence doesn't grow from thinking; it grows from movement. Real momentum starts when you let go of the idea that it has to be flawless to be valuable. Whether it's a wobbly podcast intro, a bold new business idea or finally sending the email, your next level doesn't arrive when everything's "fine-tuned." It arrives when you do.

Let this be the chapter where you stop sitting on your brilliance and start sharing it. Done isn't just good enough; it's a declaration that you're done hiding.

Confidence Cues

- Progress builds confidence, perfection delays it.
- Messy action beats perfect hesitation every single time.
- You're not behind, you're building.
- Start before you're ready. Do it scared. Do it anyway.
- Your drafts aren't wasted, they're part of your process.

"Confidence is built in the moments you choose courage over comfort."

6
Make Them Remember You

Magnetic brands are real, not curated to death!

Let me ask you something. When you walk into a networking event, a meeting, any room at all, do you walk in like you own the place? Do you walk in with your head held high, confidently, with main character energy and relaxed with a smile on your face? Or do you shrink into the background, hoping no one notices you?

Whether you realise it or not, you are showing up as your brand. The question is, are you in control and curating it, or are you accidentally letting it run the show and diluting your presence with fear, anxiety, overwhelm and no direction whatsoever?

Let me lay it down for you. The world we live in today does not need yet another perfectly polished, cookie-cutter personal brand. It needs you; unedited, unfiltered, raw and authentic, standing tall in your gorgeous heels (wobbling is allowed).

Being the brand isn't about designing a logo on Canva and spending hours obsessing about your elevator pitch. Your personal brand is the combination of how you show up to the world. It's what you are known for, the main character energy you carry and the lasting emotional impression you leave without saying a word. You might not know it yet, but your personal brand is what people need, not what you think they want.

Your personal brand is how you show up and how you make people feel. It's about becoming undeniably *you*.

So what do I really mean by *you* are the brand?

I'm talking about those signature touches that make up your unique calling card. Maybe it's the gorgeous red Chanel lipstick you wear every day. Or the Primark finds you throw together and somehow turn into high fashion. It might be your tousled hair and statement earrings that declare, "I'm creative and unapologetically myself." It's also in the way you carry yourself with shoulders back, a confident handshake and a kind smile. It's in how you listen, really listen, instead of planning your next line for the hot guy in the pink shirt standing beside you.

This chapter is about you learning to own your personal brand authentically. Before you say, "But I'm not running a business," let me stop you right there, my love. This isn't just for entrepreneurs. If you're climbing the corporate ladder, returning to the workplace or even figuring out your next move, personal branding still matters. Why? Because your brand is how people experience you, in meetings, on LinkedIn, during presentations and even in WhatsApp groups. Whether you're leading a team, interviewing for a promotion or finding your footing after years of putting everyone else first, your brand gives you back your voice. This is your reminder that you don't need a business to build a powerful reputation. You need clarity, courage and a message that reflects who you really are, not just your job title.

This is about being true to yourself, your needs and your desires, so the right people see you, remember you and want what you're offering. It's no longer about chasing perfection or feeling too scared to show up as your real, quirky self.

Because magnetic brands are real, not curated to death!

It's time, my love, to become unforgettable.

So you might be thinking, "Do I really need a personal brand?" My answer? Yes, and here's why.

Whether you're an entrepreneur, a team leader or making a midlife pivot, your personal brand is your power. It helps people understand who you are, what you stand for and why they should trust you. Visibility leads to opportunity. Not having a brand means people will define you by default; it's human nature, and what others come up with likely won't capture your brilliance. So, if you've ever felt overlooked, undervalued or like you're shouting into the brain fog, chances are your brand isn't doing you justice, yet. Let's change that.

When you don't show up as the unapologetic, authentic, raw, real version of you, you blend into a sea of sameness. You and your brand fade into the background, instantly forgotten. Each time you hide behind faceless carousel posts and stock videos, when you edit your message to sound more "realistic," and every time you wrap yourself in an invisible cloak to avoid being seen and heard, you rob your audience of the magnetic, brilliant version of you – your humanness.

Ask yourself, "What would the consequences be if I finally find the courage to back myself and show up fully aligned with who I truly am, without fear of being judged?" Let me let you in on a secret: What happens is that everything shifts.

When you finally back yourself and show up as your unapologetic midlife self, people notice. You become the woman who lights up a Zoom room without even speaking. Your message resonates because people feel your energy shift and your confidence becomes contagious. You no longer have to chase clients; opportunities find their way to you. Confidence becomes your magnet. You don't need to over-explain your worth; your energy says it for you. Sometimes it's the Chanel lipstick, tousled hair or that killer blazer you love, not to impress but to express. Other times, it's the way you truly listen, ask the thoughtful question no one else asks, or remember the detail they didn't expect you to.

You're no longer invisible. You're unforgettable.

We don't wait to be chosen. We don't wait for an invitation to someone else's table. We create our own by showing up as our true, authentic selves – quirks and all. Every day.

So, ask yourself, "Am I willing to risk staying invisible for the comfort of blending in? Or is today the day I become impossible to ignore?"

To help you really get to the bones of what I'm saying, I'll share with you some examples of high-profile women who didn't wait to be chosen. Women who stopped blending in. Women who chose themselves. Women who chose confidence and became wildly successful as a consequence, no matter their age.

Ashley Graham

Embraced her curves and became a body confidence pioneer.

Early in her career, Ashley Graham tried to blend in and fit the traditional modelling mould. But after constant rejection and disappointment, she flipped the script and embraced her curves. She went on to become a powerful advocate for body positivity, courageously appearing on the cover of *Sports Illustrated's* swimsuit edition as their first plus-size model. On social media, she shares unfiltered, unedited photos of her body, stretch marks and all, constantly challenging beauty standards. Over time, Ashley has built a brand around authentic beauty and confidence, regularly speaking on body image and self-acceptance. She even launched her own lingerie line for all sizes – a powerful example of a woman owning her story.

Brené Brown

Studies vulnerability, courage, shame and empathy. Her work has inspired millions to embrace imperfection.

In her early career as a professor, Brené Brown tried to stay in her lane as an academic researcher. But when she shared her story in a TED Talk on shame and imperfection, her career took an entirely new direction. By embracing her introversion and imperfection, she flipped the narrative, turning vulnerability into her superpower. She went on to publish several bestsellers, including *Daring Greatly* and *The Gifts of Imperfection*, which later led to her own Netflix show. A brilliant example of a woman embracing her authentic humanness.

Pink

The stage name of Alecia Beth Moore-Hart. Known for her acrobatic stage presence and activism.

Pink never fit the mould of a traditional pop star, and she pushed back hard against music labels that tried to change her. From early on, she embraced her punk-rock style and wrote songs that told her truth. "Don't Let Me Get Me" even calls out the industry pressure directly. She turned her anti-pop-star edge into a powerful brand, inspiring generations of women to embrace their "different" and own their quirks. Today, as a double-platinum award-winning artist with over 135 million records sold worldwide, Pink continues to speak unapologetically about societal expectations.

Oprah Winfrey

Known for her real human connection, Oprah became a billionaire and global icon by transcending traditional media and building an authentic personal brand.

Oprah created the *Oprah Winfrey Show* after being told she didn't fit the image of a "hard" television anchor. She embraced her struggles with her weight and childhood trauma and publicly turned her vulnerabilities into her brand superpower. Her media empire is based on honest conversations and deep human connections.

Sara Blakely

The billionaire Spanx founder who sold underwear from her living room.

Sara Blakely owned her brand from the start, famously wearing her Spanx underwear beneath her presentation outfits to prove the results. For years, she wasn't taken seriously in the male-dominated business world, but she refused to conform to corporate norms. Instead, she leaned into her quirky style with humour and humility, turning her storytelling into powerful, relatable marketing. Sara became the youngest self-made female billionaire without help from angel investors. She built her brand around real women with real bodies, solving the everyday undergarment problems they face.

Rachael Lawrence (Me!)

The founder who refused to accept she wasn't capable of more.

From reading some of my story in previous chapters, you've probably gathered that I never fit into the corporate world, and I didn't cope well with the politics of independent business either. In my early twenties, I was bullied in almost every job I held by weak women leaders, which left me doubting whether true female advocacy and leadership even existed. Then came a year that broke me wide open: miscarriage, divorce, the loss of my beloved nan and donating my kidney – all followed by a mental breakdown that tested my resilience in ways most people will never know.

But my breakdown became my biggest breakthrough. Unemployed, broke and a single mum to a toddler, I had to pick myself up off the floor (literally). I realised I no longer had the capacity to tolerate another woman's toxicity or dim my light to make someone else feel powerful. So I chose to blaze my own trail with raw determination. I went on to build several successful businesses, including Confident As Fck Coaching*, helping women across the globe. I've self-published books, launched a podcast and carved out a brand rooted in radical authenticity and empathy.

The cost was some of the most painful experiences of my life, but the wisdom I gained fuels the message I share: My voice is important, my work is worthy and my purpose is clear. Today, I'm grateful to have found my purpose of helping women own their story, rise with unshakeable confidence and build lives and businesses that feel like home.

And this is what I truly want for you, too.

It's time for you to declare to yourself and the world what you want to become known for. It's time for you to step into your visibility and become your brand.

Here's a journal exercise to help get you started.

This is your opportunity to step aside from your limiting beliefs and the thought patterns you may hold about yourself. Let your intuition guide you. It's time for you to take up space because if you don't decide what you want to be known for, the world will assign you a label, and chances are, it'll be the watered-down version of who you really are.

Exercise

Step 1: Create Your Brand Identity Declaration

Define what you want to become known for. This is your bold and unapologetic statement of what you stand for.

When people mention your name in a room you're not in, what do you want them to say?

Here are some examples to inspire you:

> She's the go-to coach for women ready to reset their mindset and build authentic brands.

She's the award-winning author and podcast host in the women's leadership space.

She's so inspiring. Every time I hear her speak, I feel so motivated to take action.

She's the woman who teaches visibility and confidence in the boardroom.

She's the woman who teaches how to self-publish books and become a best-selling author.

She's the woman who comes in and declutters and makes your house feel like a show home.

She's the woman who designs bold jewellery pieces to be passed down through the generations.

Step 2: Craft Your Brand Promise

This is where your brand becomes a promise, not just a presence. What results do you deliver? What transformation can people expect when they interact with you, work with you or consume your content?

Think of this as the "big promise" of your business or brand. What's the clear, tangible before and after you help create?

Ask yourself:

What problems am I helping people solve?

How do their lives or businesses improve because of their interaction with me?

What transformation will they experience when they complete a journey with me? What will we celebrate at the end?

Examples:

> "I help midlife women reset their mindset and rise with unshakable confidence, building businesses and brands that feel like home."

> "I empower women to overcome imposter syndrome and boldly claim their space as thought leaders in their industry."

> "I guide female entrepreneurs to step into their visibility and create irresistible personal brands and become known, seen, and sought-after, without selling their souls."

____

____

____

____

____

This promise becomes your brand declaration statement, your roadmap. Every piece of content you create, every program you offer, every conversation you have should point back to this.

Step 3: Audit Your Current Brand Presence

Now that you know what you stand for and what you promise, it's time to ask, "Is that what's coming across?"

Audit questions:

Do my social media profiles, website and content clearly communicate my brand promise?

Am I showing up visually as the next-level version of myself? Think brand colours, imagery and personal style.

Does my content speak to the transformation I create, or am I just adding to the noise?

Are my offers, pricing and messaging aligned with the brand promise I've just written?

This is where you take a bird's eye view and bring everything into alignment.

Step 4: Embody the Energy of Your Brand Promise

Your brand isn't just a message; it's an energy that people feel when they experience you.

Morning power prompt: "How would the most magnetic version of me, who fully lives and breathes my brand promise, show up today?"

Would you speak with more conviction? Finally, write the imperfect blog post because it serves your audience rather than strokes your ego? Wear the leopard print top? Attend the networking event? Start your own writing group?

Remember, your brand promise means nothing if people can't feel it when you walk into the room, open your mouth or hit "send." Be the living, breathing, walking embodiment of the transformation you offer – if that requires leopard print, then go for it!

Wear the outfit that makes you feel like a boss, even if you're only heading to the shops. Leopard print and statement earrings are not reserved for "important days."

Update your Instagram bio or LinkedIn headline to reflect what you really want to be known for: Ditch the fluff and say the thing.

Record a 60-second story or reel sharing your real reason for doing what you do. No polish. Or perfection, just authentic passion.

Take one aligned action today that the next-level you would take: Book the networking event, send the pitch, speak up in the meeting, even if your voice shakes.

Write your Brand Identity Declaration and stick it on your mirror. Read it every morning like the powerhouse you are.

Let me share a story of a client who did exactly this work.

When Emily first came to me in spring 2023, she was caught in the anxious, confusing loop so many brilliant midlife women find themselves in. On paper, she was wildly qualified. In reality, she felt like a fraud and was afraid to show up as her true self for fear of judgment and disapproval.

Juggling family life, she longed to return to her professional environment but had held back from senior banking roles for years. She convinced herself she wasn't ready for full-time work, let alone a board-level position.

As she put it: "Who am I to sit at a boardroom table? No one will take me seriously. I've been part-time for a year!"

But everything changed when she stopped hiding behind those fears and started doing the inner work to dismantle her imposter syndrome. She defined what she wanted to be known for: a calm, decisive leader who pairs deep banking compliance expertise with practical problem-solving, bringing clarity to her department and building empowered, high-performing teams.

She wrote her brand promise and began owning it in every conversation. She showed up with the energy of already having the board role; calm, quiet and assertive.

The result? She landed a board-level position at a bank she once believed was completely out of her league. She walked into the role with old doubts rising up, but this time she had the tools to manage them.

She knew exactly who she needed to embody to deserve that seat at the table she had once thought was reserved for "someone better."

Within a year, she doubled her salary, earned the respect of the executive team, and most importantly, found the balance she had been craving: fulfilled as a mum, wife and senior executive in a career she had curated for herself. She found her people and her place.

This is the power of showing up as your brand. You don't just change how the world sees you. You get to be in charge of your circumstances, and that's where the magic happens.

It's time now for you to choose yourself. You're ready to be seen and remembered.

Final Thoughts

You're not building a personal brand to impress people; you're building one to express who you really are.

Not the polished version. Not the version you think will be accepted. The real you: your story, your energy, your unapologetic essence. That's the magic people remember. You don't have to chase attention; you just need to show up with clarity and conviction about what you stand for.

Whether you're running a business, making a career pivot or stepping back into your power after years of playing small, your brand is already speaking for you. The only question is, are you writing the message or letting the noise write it for you?

The most magnetic thing you can be is fully, fiercely yourself. The world doesn't need another carbon copy.

It needs the authentic woman who finally decided she was enough, exactly as she is, and showed up like it.

Confidence Cues

- You are the brand. Own it before anyone else can.
- Magnetic confidence starts with authentic expression.
- Stop waiting to be "ready." Start showing up as you.

- Visibility isn't vanity, it's leadership.

- Your quirks are your signature. Lean into them, not out.

"Owning your worth isn't arrogance; it's survival. And it's power."

7
Own Your Worth

If I had a fiver for every woman who has come to me and said, "My passion is helping people. I just want to help as many people as I can," and then goes on to skip asking for the pay rise or undercharges for her services, I'd be sipping an ice-cold glass of Veuve Clicquot on my Sunseeker in St. Tropez by now.

I'm going to get straight to the point. Owning your worth is a non-negotiable. Whether you're a stay-at-home mum, a corporate leader, a coach or a consultant considering your next move, it's time to start recognising the value of your life. By that, I mean your time, skills and presence have a unique value and you get to decide what that looks like in terms of price. But more than this, raising your rates and owning your worth is about boundaries, respect and unapologetic confidence in who you are and what you bring to the table.

If you keep undercharging for your work and your worth based on what you think the industry "standard" is or what you think people can afford, you will forever remain at a threshold that seems impossible to smash through.

It's not just about earning less. It's about losing more time, energy and self-respect. When we stay silent, we stay stuck. We carry that frustration into our homes, our bodies and our relationships. You start to second-guess yourself in every room you walk into and this ends up bleeding into your confidence. You might not notice it straight away, but eventually you find yourself shrinking, taking on more than you should, feeling resentful and wondering why everyone else seems to be racing ahead while you feel as though you're stuck in the same place.

You can't live an exceptional life with "just enough." You certainly won't live the life of your dreams by constantly discounting your value in your career and in your head!

In this chapter, you'll understand why charging for what you're worth or asking for a raise is one of the most radical acts of self-respect and leadership you can make. You'll finally stop undervaluing yourself, whether that's in your business, career or personal life.

Value is *energy,* not just *exchange.* When you ask for a pay rise or charge more than someone else in your niche, you elevate not only how others perceive you, but how you perceive yourself. This isn't about being greedy. The exchange is about everything you bring to the table, your experiences, wisdom, intuition and years of fine-tuning your art. All of which has a huge amount of unique value. It's about time we unlock it.

You're not on your own in undermining your worth. In fact, most women have been conditioned from a young age to feel guilty about asking for more, whether that's more money, more recognition or simply more space to stand in our power.

The numbers prove it. A UK survey revealed that 45% of women feel they are underpaid, while at the very same time, 67% of men said they were content with their current salary.[8] That's almost half of women believing they're not being valued fairly, while two-thirds of men feel satisfied with what they're earning. I mean, what the actual FUCK?!

This isn't about capability, it's about conditioning. When women are taught to "be grateful" rather than to negotiate, self-advocate or push back, we internalise the idea that wanting more is somehow wrong. The truth? Wanting more is not greed. It's growth. And until we normalise asking for what we deserve, this gap between how women and men experience their worth will keep repeating.

But it goes deeper than that. Women have never been encouraged to talk about money, and historically, it has been a taboo subject. It is often considered crass to speak openly about the value we bring to the table and how much we are paid for it. In many cultures, women are socialised to be more modest and less assertive, which makes asking for a raise feel risky. They fear rocking the boat with colleagues or employers or facing negative consequences that could affect future opportunities. These deep-seated beliefs are costing us dearly.

Undercharging and undervaluing yourself means you feel like you are stuck in a rut, with more month than money. Let's be honest here. "More month than money" isn't just a cute phrase; it's bloody awful when you're living it. It means checking your bank balance before you say yes to a coffee date. It means putting things back at checkout because payday is still two weeks away. It's the knot in your stomach when the direct debits come out and there's more red than black on your account screen. And this isn't because you're lazy or unqualified. It's because imposter syndrome has left you playing small for too damn long, undercharging and undervaluing yourself out of habit, not reality, instead of building wealth and progressing. Constantly attracting clients, projects and jobs that drain you instead of energising you, and worse still, if you're anything like I was, you're modelling undervaluing to your daughters, colleagues and friends.

Not having hard conversations with yourself and facing your fears or limiting beliefs around money will likely cause you more exhaustion, burnout and resentment over time. Even worse, you may never reach your financial or personal potential, and as you know by now, we're no longer available for that!

I promise you the moment you decide to flip the script on what you are worth is the moment you magnetise better opportunities, stop overworking and start leading and experiencing more joy and freedom. You are no longer stuck in fear and, worse still, survival mode. You no longer allow pesky negative thoughts around money to surface because you know how to shut down your inner bitch critic and move forward, asking for what you want with clarity and confidence.

I know that a promise is a big statement, but I also know it's true: I've experienced it myself and so have many of my clients.

In 2011, I was asked by a large mental health organisation to host several mental health first aid training sessions for a local council. The rate they were offering to pay me was very low. There was extensive travel involved, and by the time I netted the numbers, it just wasn't going to be financially viable for me. But the opportunity was *huge*. My fear was that if I asked for more, they would go elsewhere, and I would miss out on educating and helping over 700 people. At the time, for me, that was a huge number of people – the biggest project I had been offered.

I knew how much the training would benefit these people, and whilst I understood the knock-on effect of educating them in mental health first aid strategies was not something you could put a monetary value on, my business wasn't a charity and the numbers had to work.

The fact of the matter was, these trainings saved lives, and I put a lot of time, energy and skill into teaching each training. I was incredibly passionate about making sure this material was delivered emphatically, knowing first-hand what it takes to recover from mental illness. Ensuring these trainings were delivered properly was very important to me.

I knew this gave me an edge that other training companies didn't have. Deep down, I understood this was my moment to really put my own coaching advice into action. I knew what I had to do.

I was trembling when I spoke to the organisation's financial lead. She was tough, and given my past experiences with female bosses, my old fears of not being good enough quickly surfaced. She told me I was lucky to be given the opportunity, as they usually worked with much larger training companies, not solopreneurs. She insisted the fee was industry standard and non-negotiable.

But my gut spoke up: "Your work isn't industry standard. It's exceptional. The transformations you create are worth backing yourself. Own your worth and see what happens."

So I did. I told her she was welcome to go to her "preferred suppliers" for industry-standard training, but if she wanted her organisation to be known as the gold standard, she needed to work with me and pay my fee, which was double what she'd offered. If she preferred mediocre training from disengaged trainers, that was her choice.

At that moment, I had to be 100% okay with the risk that she would say no. I had to back myself and trust that other opportunities would find their way to me.

It was a long 48 hours after we ended our call, and the whole time I was thinking, "Shit. Who the hell do I think I am, standing up to the head of finance like that!?" Don't get me wrong, I delivered my message well, not arrogantly or ego-led, just factually reminded her of the transformations my training had accomplished and that even though I was an independent trainer, I was the preferred supplier to a lot of companies.

The email landed with a little ping like any other, but the moment I saw her name in the subject line, my stomach dropped. I'd rehearsed this moment a hundred times in my head. I told myself it didn't matter if they said no. A massive part of me was expecting a "Thanks, but no thanks."

Instead, there it was: "We'd love to go ahead." With the contract and the new, doubled rate in black and white. I swear I had to read it three times. She hadn't tried to negotiate me down again. She had accepted it. My rate. The one I had nearly talked myself out of. I sat there in shock, hands shaking slightly, heart thudding with adrenaline and pride. For once, I hadn't crumbled. I had spoken my worth into the room, and the universe mirrored it right back to me. That email wasn't just a booking. It was a deeply personal, monumental, fucking breakthrough. Proof that when we stop seeking validation and start standing our ground, everything changes. I knew I'd done it. For once, I stood up to an intimidating woman, I didn't back down and it paid off.

When the project was over and the feedback came in, the organisation was thrilled. It was the first time they had received a 100% positive feedback response from any of their training. It was a powerful lesson for both of us and one that cemented in me the undeniable power of backing yourself and not compromising on your standards.

And it didn't end there. With every new project I was offered, I found myself confidently asking for more. Sometimes it was money, but often it was extra time, a better training venue, or more administrative support. The opportunities kept coming, and I was able to deliver this much-needed training to more people.

The crazy thing is, when you truly value yourself, you attract people who are happy to pay your rate. The same applies when you're negotiating a pay rise. Most people lead with ego-driven reasons, which only get people's backs up. But if you come prepared with numbers, facts, feedback and hard evidence, it's very difficult for your boss to say no. Remember, it costs far more to replace you with the advertising, hiring and training involved than it does to keep you. That is your bargaining power, so use it.

I've seen this confidence play out with my daughter, too. Her working career started in hospitality, and she was on the standard hourly rate, which was fine. But, months later, when she was offered a different position working from home for another company, filling staff vacancies for a care organisation, they offered her significantly more money. This became her financial and energetic standard. So when a local boutique asked her to work with them a couple of days a week and they suggested their hourly rate, she didn't miss a beat! She politely thanked them for the wonderful opportunity and said, "I'd love to work with you, but my skills in negotiation and sales are worth more than that."

And they loved that. They matched her salary with the organisation she was currently working for, which was a higher-than-normal retail standard. She is now one of their best-selling advisors, regularly selling their most expensive items! Can you imagine having that confidence at 18 years old? Can you imagine instilling that kind of confidence in yourself? In your daughters? In every woman that you know? It's such a powerful lesson for us all. Life is expensive. Why should we have to lose out just because of our conditioning around what we are worth?

If I had continued to allow my old conditioning around money and self-worth to be my energetic standard, this book might never have been written because I wouldn't have been able to afford to set aside time to write it. I also don't write books purely for financial reasons. I write them because I know my words and wisdom can help people. That is my focus.

You've heard me share in my personal story how I didn't justify my price. I simply spoke candidly about the transformation my training provided, and that was the key that unlocked the door to me receiving more. And it's not just me, let me share an example that might just sound like you.

Samira is a mindset and self-worth coach who came to me at the back end of 2022, when she was in her late 30s, because her business felt energetically stuck. She was constantly fully booked but still financially stretched. Every time she looked at her calendar, she felt overwhelmed. She was delivering high-touch transformation but charging low rates, and it was burning her out.

We looked at her offers and pricing together, and it was clear she was undercharging massively. When I asked her why she hadn't raised her prices, she said, "I'm scared I'll lose clients. I just want to help people who really need it." Sound familiar?

I reminded her of something she'd forgotten: Your clients can only rise as high as the energetic standard you have set for yourself. So we did some work and she decided to be brave.

Samira didn't just raise her rates; she introduced a tiered pricing structure. She offered three levels of support, clearly showing the transformation at each stage. Her new structure empowered clients to choose what level of support they needed and take ownership of their investment. They still had skin in the game and felt supported.

Obviously, she still felt nervous when she first sent out a proposal with the new rates. She second-guessed herself the moment she hit send. But you know what happened? Her client said yes to the top-tier package. And then another one did. And another.

Samira's income increased substantially in three months. But more than that, she started to feel expansive again. She believed in her offers more than ever, because she wasn't undervaluing the energy, wisdom and transformation she brought to the table. She no longer felt burnt out or ready to throw in the towel.

As she told me later, "It stopped being about what I was charging. It became about how deeply I believed in what I offer."

And that's the secret sauce that takes the fear out of asking for more.

When you stop pricing for your purse and price for your clients' transformation, or when you take ownership of a project at work and step into more responsibility or leadership, your results will have an impact. You will be seen as the go-to expert in that field, and you will feel more comfortable receiving the remuneration you deserve. You are not responsible for other people's money stories; you're responsible for delivering transformation. Equally, if you are an entrepreneur considering raising your rates, if your clients don't have skin in the game, they don't show up for the transformation you offer.

When you focus on outcomes and transformations, then you have a winning formula for raising your rates.

Your prices or hourly rates reflect your self-belief. If you undervalue yourself, you'll attract jobs, opportunities and people who do the same, because the world pays you at the level you believe you deserve.

If you've been nodding along thinking, "Yes, I know I need to ask for a pay rise or charge more…but I still feel stuck", this is where I want you to take a breath and get brutally honest with yourself. Cut through the noise. Your rates are only one piece of the worth puzzle. You could double your fees tomorrow, but if the way you negotiate, set boundaries or choose opportunities is still rooted in undervaluing yourself, the cracks will show.

I want you to see the full picture of how you're valuing yourself from a money and worth perspective, not just on paper, but in your daily choices.

Now this is where the Money & Worth Alignment Wheel comes in.

This isn't about life balance or ticking boxes. This is about pulling back the curtain on the subtle (and not-so-subtle) ways you might be undercharging, over-delivering or saying yes to things that keep you underpaid, overworked and undervalued.

Money & Worth Alignment Wheel

Find out where you are fully in your worth and where you are settling.

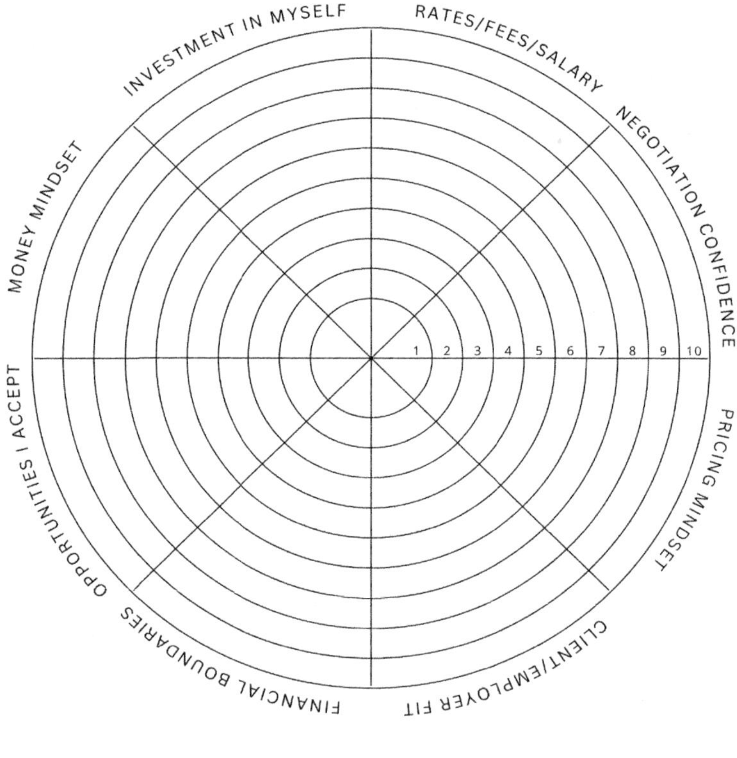

How to Use the Wheel

Shade the segments in each section of the wheel from the centre outwards, giving yourself a score from 1 to 10 where 1 (in the centre) means "completely out of alignment" and 10 (on the outer edge) means "fully aligned." Be brutally honest. No one else is going to see this but you.

Take a look at the questions below related to each section of the wheel to help you decide how aligned you currently are.

Write in your scores for each segment and circle the lowest-scoring statement. This is your biggest money-and-worth leak.

Rates/Fees/Salary – Am I charging/earning what I'm worth?

YOUR SCORE: ______________________________

Negotiation Confidence – Do I ask for more without apology?

YOUR SCORE: ______________________________

Pricing Mindset – Am I pricing for my value, not my wallet?

YOUR SCORE: ____________________________________

Client/Employer Fit – Do they see and respect my value?

YOUR SCORE: ____________________________________

Financial Boundaries – Do I protect my time and scope?

YOUR SCORE: ____________________________________

Opportunities I Accept – Are they aligned with my worth?

YOUR SCORE: ____________________________________

Money Mindset – Do I believe I deserve more?

YOUR SCORE: ____________________________________

Investment in Myself – Do I put money back into my growth?

YOUR SCORE: ____________________________

For the section where you scored lowest, finish the sentence below with a bold, unapologetic statement that will help you to become more aligned in that area.

I give myself permission to….

____

____

____

Now I'd like you to grab your journal and answer these questions with unapologetic honesty. This is your mirror moment.

Look at the segment you scored lowest in on the Money & Worth Alignment Wheel. Where exactly am I undercharging, under-asking or undervaluing myself right now? Think about rates, salary, client fees or boundaries around your time and energy.

____

____

How does that make me feel?

____

____

What beliefs or stories am I holding that tell me I can't ask for more?

____

____

Where have I been pricing for my own wallet instead of my client's transformation or undervaluing the results I deliver at work?

____

____

What's the real cost of my staying in this pattern? Time, energy, resentment, financial strain?

____

____

If I truly believed in my worth, what would I ask for? Write the number down. Own it.

____

____

Where do I need stronger boundaries to support this next-level version of me?

____

____

Commit, right now, to take one bold, high-value action this week that moves you closer to the life and income you desire. Don't just read this – *do* this.

A more detailed guide and template for the Money & Worth Alignment Wheel Template can be found on my website. Instructions are in the conclusion of this book.

Money & Worth Alignment Wheel Template

The Money & Worth Alignment Wheel is here to help you spot where you're leaking money and self-worth so you can seal the gaps and step into abundance.

Download your printable wheel at rachaellawrence.co.uk/book-bonuses using the password BOOKBONUSES. It's totally free, so make sure you don't miss out. You can also scan the QR code to get access.

Book Bonuses

SCAN ME

Final Thoughts

Your worth is not a question mark; it's a full stop. It's the baseline you decide on, not something to be earned, negotiated or endlessly explained.

Every time you say yes to being underpaid, overworked or overlooked, you send a message to the world and to yourself that your value is flexible. It isn't. Your time, your energy, your brilliance and your years of lived experience hold serious weight.

This chapter isn't just about money; it's about reclaiming the power that comes when you stop settling. Because the moment you decide you're no longer available for the bare minimum – whether that's in respect, of rates or recognition – is the moment the game changes. Raise the standard, and everything around you will rise to meet it. This isn't entitlement. This is self-respect in action, and it's long overdue.

So ask for more. Charge your worth. Lead with confidence. And watch your transformation meet you at your new, energetic expectation.

Confidence Cues

- Owning your worth is not arrogance; it's alignment.
- If you don't value yourself, neither will they.
- Confidence sounds like: "This is my rate." Full stop.
- Money mirrors your mindset. Upgrade both.

- You don't ask for permission to rise; you claim the damn space.

- When you price for transformation (not your own wallet), your clients and employers take you seriously.

- Remember: You are not responsible for other people's money stories. You are responsible for honouring your values.

"The day you stop asking for permission is the day you become unstoppable."

8
The CEO of Your Life

If you're not the one in the driver's seat, switching into gear, with your sat nav pointing at your north star, then you're probably sat in the back, holding the snacks whilst someone else decides where your life is heading.

It's time to take back the wheel, love.

I hope you've realised it by now, but this isn't just another book about "overcoming imposter syndrome." It's so much more than that. This book and the work you have been doing are about taking complete responsibility for your life and future.

You are no longer waiting for a promotion to be offered to you. You're not waiting for the big wide world to discover you and you're most definitely not waiting for someone else to validate your potential.

In this chapter, you will discover that *you* are the CEO of your life, and that means *you* run the show.

This chapter is your final call to stop with the excuses, outsourcing your power and start leading from within because you're ready.

I know you are ready and deep down, I know you know you are too.

This chapter is where we start to dig deep into what it really means to live authentically, quieten the imposter syndrome noise and act like you are the CEO of your life. I promise no boring grey suit is required!

Whether you're a founder, a freelancer or a full-time employee, the world doesn't need another cookie-cutter blueprint.

It needs you, your presence, your unique skillset and experiences, your wisdom and your personality.

So, What Does It Mean to Be the CEO of Your Life?

Let's get one thing clear. I'm not talking about pretty social media quotes and an aesthetically pleasing Pinterest board or a beautifully curated Louis Vuitton planner.

Being the CEO of your life means encapsulating an entire way of being.

It means facing your fears and moving through them anyway. It means looking at your life as a whole, every facet that makes you who you are and taking radical responsibility for it all: your time, energy, money, relationships and choices.

It means no longer running to the latest guru in your industry or to ChatGPT for answers, but instead trusting your gut and listening to your intuition.

You don't wait for someone to stamp your hand with approval to enter this phase of your life.

You get to decide. You make the hard decisions, and you move. You adjust your sail and pivot when you need to. That could be leaving a job you have outgrown or a relationship that has run its course. It could mean quietly walking away from a toxic friendship or standing up to people who think they are in charge of you.

You define what success looks like for you – not your husband's, your mum's or your best mate's version, but yours. Maybe it's building a seven-figure brand, or maybe it's picking your kids up from school every day and never missing bedtime. It's your call. Being the CEO of your life means making executive decisions not from fear or people-pleasing, but from alignment with your values, your vision and your truth.

When you don't take the driver's seat, you drift through life saying yes to everything that drains you. You keep spinning plates until you are so exhausted you cannot tell what day it is, and eventually you crash and burn. All the people pleasing, procrastinating, over-forgiving, doing what everyone else wants and undercharging pile up into one big ball of resentment. You begin to resent the people you follow online who seem to have it all together, and worse, you resent yourself. In five years, you may look back and ask, "Whose life have I been living?"

But when you step back into the driver's seat and step up as the CEO, this is where you return to your authenticity.

You begin to work in alignment because you have crystal clarity. You stop sense-checking yourself with people who may not share your vision, and instead let your desire and determination take over. You stop outsourcing your power and return to yourself, knowing you already hold the answers within. You are no longer dragged along by life; you begin to curate and design the life you want. You make your choices with confidence, taking high-level, CEO-worthy risks outside your comfort zone. This time, your decisions are not driven by fear of getting it wrong, but by full ownership and leadership of your life.

This is not just about what you do anymore. It's who you need to become when you take the reins.

This era of your life is about working in full alignment with your values and no longer being so afraid that you cannot do the very thing that will take you to your next level. The level you have been craving for so long.

Forget corporate KPIs (Key Performance Indicators). What you need are PPIs (Personal Performance Indicators), because this is your life and it deserves to be audited accordingly.

At the start of 2024, I rolled into the new year feeling completely untethered, overwhelmed, unsure and quietly terrified. Deep down, I knew what was going on, but up until that point, I hadn't found the courage to face it.

I was standing at a crossroads, one that stretched across both my career and my relationship with my now-husband, Alistair. The universe was nudging (okay, shoving) me to make some big decisions. And honestly? I didn't want to make them. I was scared. Scared of committing. Scared of getting it wrong. Scared that if I chose one path, I was closing the door on another.

But I eventually realised that the fear wasn't really about what I had to do. It was about who I had to become.

Committing fully to myself and my career meant owning my ambition again. It meant learning new skills, showing up online and declaring to my friends, family and clients that I was experiencing another pivot, and that scared me. Committing fully to my relationship meant being vulnerable in a way that didn't come naturally to me. Allowing a man to see this vulnerability when I was experiencing so many mental and physical changes made me incredibly nervous. I felt like I was stripping away all of my safety barriers. I mean, what's sexy about a walking, talking, nervous wreck?

Alistair and I had been doing long distance for a while, with 360 miles between us. One of us was always either in the car or on a plane, and while that felt romantic at the start, it soon became clear we could not do it forever. At the same time, my work had started to feel stale. I couldn't put my finger on it at first, but eventually, I saw it for what it was: I had outgrown it. I was no longer excited or inspired. I knew I needed to pivot, but the idea of reinventing myself again felt both freeing and paralysing.

So, I did the one thing I always do when shit gets real. I turned inwards.

I began some deep mindset work and daily journaling. What started as scattered notes of self-reflection slowly became something more structured and powerful. I reconnected with my values and my bigger dream for my life. Somewhere between those scribbled thoughts and quiet morning meditations, the fog began to lift.

Alistair was incredibly supportive during this time. He showed up for me in every way I had ever wanted a partner to. But even then, I had to make the choice to fully let him in. I had to trust him, and trust does not come easily to me. Years of online dating will do that.

Nine months later, I made the biggest executive decision of my life. I packed up my things, moved to Scotland, and stayed with Alistair and his two children, while my daughter Ella remained behind to finish her A-levels. It was the hardest thing I have ever done, but also the clearest sign that I was finally acting from alignment rather than fear.

By then, those journal entries and mindset musings in my notes app had turned into something I never expected: a book.

I decided to publish *Reset Your Mind* on 1 January 2025. The date felt symbolic: self-publishing a book for women everywhere as a declaration that this is the year we stop shrinking. *Reset Your Mind* is a step-by-step roadmap to rediscover your purpose, overcome mindset blocks and design a life you love. It is not your average self-help book. It is raw, practical and rooted in my own experience of navigating depression, anxiety and starting over from scratch. Think of it as a reset button for your entire mindset, complete with real coaching tools, journaling prompts and empowering practices to guide you out of survival mode and into alignment.

Did the imposter syndrome try to sabotage me? Of course it did. The whispers from my inner bitch voice of "Who do you think you are?" were loud. But I felt the fear and did it anyway. Just weeks after releasing the book, I finally had the breakthrough I'd been waiting for. I knew exactly where I was heading next.

I was going to help midlife women. Women who, like me, were facing a thousand invisible pivots and wondering if it was too late to start again. Women who had spent years supporting everyone else and suddenly realised they'd become invisible in their own story. Women sitting on wisdom, life lessons and brilliance, but who had no idea how to package it, publish it or speak it out loud.

That's when I made the pivot into visibility coaching.

At 45, I claimed my space as a visibility mentor, ICF-certified coach, author and podcast host. My work now focuses on helping midlife women share the comeback story they were destined to tell. I guide them in turning their wisdom into an unforgettable book, brand and platform that not only generates income but also creates impact and legacy.

If you are battling self-doubt, imposter syndrome or the gut feeling that you have outgrown your current life but do not know how to begin your next chapter, I see you. And I can help. Think of it as brand visibility, storytelling and confidence mentorship for women ready to share their midlife comeback story, elevate their professional presence and take up space unapologetically. No fluff. No filters. Just fierce, founder-led content, strategy, mindset coaching and positioning work that actually moves the needle. I created this for the woman who knows she has something important to say, yet still finds herself stuck behind the scenes, doubting her worth and playing small online.

Through my signature blend of mindset coaching, storytelling mentorship and visibility strategy, I help women reset their identity, reclaim their voice and rise with confidence on the page, online and in real life.

It's still in its infancy, but it's alive, and it's me. A brand built not from a polished business plan, but from experience, emotion and embodiment. It never would've happened if I hadn't made the brave decision to reset my mind in 2024, reflect on my values and what work felt aligned in my midlife era and step into unknown territory with my whole heart.

And Alistair? Well, I did the thing I said I wasn't going to do. I married him. We had a beautiful, simple ceremony in

Edinburgh with just two friends as witnesses. No frills, no fuss, just love, laughter and a deep sense of mutual respect.

Marriage didn't feel like a box to tick this time. It felt like a conscious choice. A co-creation. A new chapter that honoured our pasts but was rooted firmly in the present. It was a reminder that the most powerful decisions in life are the ones you make from a place of full-hearted alignment, not fear, not obligation, not pressure, just love, courage and clarity.

Journal Exercise

Where in my life am I avoiding a big decision out of fear?
•
•
•
•
•

What would the CEO version of me choose instead?
•
•
•
•
•

What really matters to me (e.g. my free time, peace of mind, making an impact, leaving a legacy)?
•
•
•
•
•

Reflecting on my values and beyond money, what does success look like for me?
•   •   •   •   •

Where am I trying to lead from masculine energy?
•   •   •   •   •

What would happen if I soften into trust?
•
•
•
•
•

Once you have this clarity, allow it to become your sat nav. Not your fears or your imposter syndrome!

Starting today, I want you to ask yourself, "Would the CEO version of me spend an hour scrolling on Instagram? Or would she mindfully choose to go for a walk? Would she spend a week avoiding the pricing conversation or the pay rise meeting? Or would she make arranging the meeting her top priority? Would she wait for someone else to notice her value or would she write it in 14 font size, underline and bold it?"

These seemingly small choices ultimately build bold identities.

Leading in your midlife isn't about hustle and grind. It's about emotional intelligence, intuition and creating space for joy.

You don't need to hustle harder. We're no longer available for that! You need to lead more softly. Accept that it's time, and perfectly okay for you to lead with your intuition, creativity, collaboration and flow. This means knowing when to push and when to pause. When to rise and when to rest. This is your new CEO leadership framework. It's time to trust that it works.

Final Thoughts

You are not here to live by default. You're here to live by design.

Being the CEO of your life is about knowing what matters to you, making intentional decisions and taking full ownership of where you're headed next. It means being honest about what's working, what isn't and where you've been handing your power over without realising it.

You don't need to please everyone, follow the crowd or have all the answers. You just need to start trusting yourself more deeply and acting in alignment with your values, not your doubts. By now, I hope you are starting to understand this isn't about perfection. It's about progress that feels right to you.

You get to define success on your own terms and create a life that reflects who you truly are. That clarity? That quiet conviction? It changes everything. Keep choosing what's true for you, and let the rest fall away.

You don't need a corporate title to lead like a CEO. You already have the wisdom, the instincts, the vision.

You've always had it. Now it's time to own it.

Confidence Cues

- You're the CEO of your life. Act like it.
- Alignment over approval, always.
- You don't need permission to pivot.
- Audit your energy like a boss. What drains, what fuels?
- Lead your life like it matters, because it does.

"Stop shrinking. You weren't built for the sidelines—you were built for the spotlight."

9

Stay in Your Power

When you start showing up for yourself and shining brighter, don't be surprised that some people reach for their sunglasses or try to switch off your light entirely. Don't let them, because girl, you've got better things to do!

Congratulations! You've reached the part of the book where it's time to celebrate. You've done some great inner work and it's time to track your wins, no matter how small, just like how a successful CEO tracks profit. Don't be in a rush to get to your next goal without acknowledging how far you've come on your journey. Even CEOs take their teams out for champagne when they hit milestones. You're the team. Pop the cork.

And just when you thought the inner work was done, don't worry, I've got you. In this chapter, we're going to talk about what happens when you start showing up differently in the world and how to hold your power when others don't quite get it yet. Because you're the CEO now, and not everyone will love the new org chart...

What I have found in my 25 years working in the life coaching and mentoring space is that often, your hardest step in transformation isn't the initial change, but maintaining it against external pressures to go back to who you were before.

This is why it is essential to learn how to stay in your power without dimming your light for the comfort or happiness of others. This means that no matter what, you must refuse to shrink back into outdated spaces or versions of you that are no longer aligned with who you are becoming – the very best version of you. It means firmly standing your ground, in your truth, even when you feel discomfort and fears bubbling up to the surface. Never mind the side eye from Aunt Doris, your boss or your closest friends.

It means when people are criticising, you don't let them cause you to go off track. You know deep down what you want and why you want it, and you're ready to make yourself and your dreams your priority.

It's time, my love, to quieten the noise, handle the pushback and attract your people because you've done the inner work. Now comes the real test: staying in your power when life (and people) try to pull you back into old patterns that no longer serve you.

As human beings, it is completely normal, when we go through a period of transformation or mindset work, to occasionally slide back into our old habits and patterns of self-doubt. This is why it is so important to stay empowered by instilling daily habits into our routines.

When you don't stay empowered, you start to lose your hard-earned confidence and momentum at crucial moments. You fall back into old habits, stay stuck in the endless cycle of fear and I-can't-handle-its, as you watch someone else overtake and step into your goals and dreams. The very dreams that *you* pinned to your vision board. And what are we not doing anymore? You've guessed it!

Instead, we are learning how to step into courage and stay in our power, attracting new friends and raving fans.

By stepping into courage, you attract supportive, inspiring relationships and become an empowering example for others. Your life becomes expansive, overflowing with fulfilment, love and happiness. Your dreams that have been pinned to your vision board start to become your reality, and this is what I mean by living in your authenticity.

I've allowed other people's opinions, narratives, criticism and fears to blindside me into changing course so many times before. And every time I've allowed it, I've wound up feeling pissed off, annoyed with myself and extremely frustrated because it's sewn seeds of doubt that have ultimately led me down a path of doubting my vision and my capabilities. It's delayed things for me. Which is not okay! So I've now learned how to stay in my power because I'm in my midlife era. I don't have time for other people's bullshit anymore. There are still big things for me to do, more women for me to help and Louis Vuitton handbags I absolutely need in my life!

But I wasn't always this empowered and strong. I wasn't always this wise. This was something that I purposely had to grow and nurture.

In 2017, I was working my ass off, saving every penny to pay for my daughter's school fees. Back then, my approach wasn't as strategic as it is today, but I was beginning to understand the power and importance of additional income streams.

I was attending property investment courses and immersed in a demanding one-year mentorship program. My life was a constant juggle: being a single mum, running my own business, commuting to London every other weekend, navigating a complicated long-distance situationship and trying to prioritise friendships.

Despite the chaos, I felt genuinely happy, fulfilled and excited for this new chapter. For the first time, I had a clear purpose and passion. I was building my dreams, and it showed. My clothes felt good on me, my confidence blossomed, and I moved into a gorgeous, brand-new apartment. Most importantly, I finally felt like I was truly providing for my daughter.

But sadly, not everyone saw my growth as a positive. Friends who I thought would celebrate with me instead mocked my efforts, talked negatively about me behind my back and even fabricated stories that turned others against me. It hurt deeply. I spent years pouring my time, energy and a fair amount of Sauvignon Blanc into these friendships, so their reactions left me confused and heartbroken. Why couldn't they celebrate my wins? Why the jealousy?

Here's the uncomfortable truth I came to realise: My growth was shining a harsh spotlight on their stagnation. It illuminated spaces in their lives where they weren't achieving, where they felt unhappy and held back by limiting beliefs and fear. They weren't ready or willing to face their own shadows, so instead, they projected their discomfort back onto me through lies, gaslighting and hurtful behaviour. One friend even openly admitted she was so jealous of me that she couldn't bear to be around me anymore. Those were her exact words! And they stung. Instead of taking inspiration from my journey, as I encourage my clients to do, she chose to tear me down, ghosting me completely and spreading false stories to justify her actions. Overnight, I lost an entire group of friends. I was left isolated and deeply hurt.

Imagine the loneliness when the early months of 2020 hit, along with a global pandemic, and I found myself utterly alone with nobody to talk to. Anger, hurt and humiliation consumed me. I'm far from perfect, but I've always prided myself on being humble, empathetic and kind, so this betrayal almost derailed me completely. I desperately tried to mend fences, but they weren't interested.

That sadness was overwhelming, and just when I thought things couldn't get worse, my seven-year situationship ended abruptly, sending me back to my kitchen floor. But amidst all of this pain and confusion, I heard a whisper. It was barely there, but I most definitely heard it. It was the voice of my intuition, gently saying, "It's okay. You're going to be okay. You've got everything you need inside of you to get through this," and in that moment, through my tear-stained face and gritted teeth, I remembered every piece of mindset work I'd done, every past experience of overcoming being torn down, belittled and gaslit by others, and I reminded myself of exactly who the fuck I was

So I went to work on rebuilding myself. I confronted the negative emotions head-on, challenged the false narratives, especially when my inner bitch voice decided to chime in, and I chose to shine brighter than ever. I walked past those former friends on the street with my head held high, ignored them confidently in the pub and built a business and brand even more successful and fulfilling than before. I transformed that pain into wisdom and strength. I turned that shit into gold.

Through it all, I learned a crucial lesson. Some people will always choose to stay exactly where they are. Even as they complain about their lives, relationships and jobs, they're not ready to do the inner work required to heal and move forward. Their coping mechanism for jealousy, low self-worth, intimidation and insecurity is tearing down the women brave enough to face their fears and heal. Women who choose growth despite discomfort.

I share this story not to boast or elevate myself but to offer you hope. When those closest to you try to dim your light because you're shining brighter, it is not your job to shrink back down. You can handle it, and *you must* handle it. Don't allow other people walking a path different from yours to derail your journey.

I chose in that horrible time to hold on to my inherent kindness, emotional intelligence, generosity and friendship boundaries like my life depended on it, because it did. And thank God I found the strength to hold firm.

Today, I stand proudly as a successful mother, wife and businesswoman, surrounded by aligned friendships rooted in love, kindness and mutual respect. We celebrate each other's wins wholeheartedly, support each other through life's ups and downs and create safe spaces for genuine connection.

When I return to my old hometown now, I see those former friends quickly ducking out of sight, unchanged and still stuck in their familiar patterns. And that's completely okay with me. I've forgiven them because their rejection became my powerful catalyst for growth. Without this test and my mindset reset, I might have settled into their stagnation and unhappiness.

Today, my mission is clear. I teach women like you how to deeply trust your wisdom, values and authenticity, and how to hold onto your power fiercely. I'm here to guide you in confidently stepping into your new, empowered self with absolute clarity and an unwavering belief that you deserve to blossom.

If there is one thing I'd like you to take from my deeply personal story, it's to expect the pushback and learn how to handle it.

Practical Concepts to Maintain Your Power

Accept that not everyone has the same beliefs, values, vision and desire that you have.

They won't always agree with what you are doing, and you may notice some relationships will change. Whether that be with your family members, work colleagues or your best mate, anticipate that some people might not be able to handle the newest, boldest version of you – and that's okay.

The key here is normalising the resistance and using it as your catalyst to keep moving forward. You don't need to, and shouldn't, internalise the criticisms. Accept that it's okay for not everyone to get it and carry on doing you anyway. (I understand this is easier said than done.)

You can do this by pausing and recognising their reactions as projections, not truths. As well as taking some deep breaths to ground you when you need to.

In moments when I am feeling challenged, I have, once again, found affirmations to be lifesavers. Here are my favourites that you may find useful:

> "I am grounded in who I am. Other people's opinions are reflections of their journey, not mine."

> "Criticism does not define me. My truth and worth remain constant, regardless of others' perceptions."

"I choose to let go of external negativity, focusing only on the growth and empowerment within me."

"I am responsible for my own happiness and success. I will not shrink or dim my light for other people's comfort."

"My confidence and authenticity are unshakable. I move forward aligned with my values and vision."

Your turn. Write a couple of affirmations you know will help you when the time comes.

Another way to maintain your power is to intentionally surround yourself with people who are on a similar journey to you. People who are expanding their beliefs around what's possible.

How to Stay in Your Power (Even on the Wobbly Days)

Start with a Safe Space to Experiment

For me, joining supportive groups and communities online really helped me find my people. I could show up as the woman I wanted to be, without fear of backlash or judgment. It became my experimental ground, somewhere I could test my voice, try new things and show up without having it all figured out. And the best bit? The people who were meant to connect with me did. The ones who didn't? Well, they quietly went about their business.

This gave me the confidence to rediscover my voice and interact in ways that felt empowering. I recommend you do the same. Seek out a space that feels good. Remind yourself of hobbies you used to enjoy or if there is something new you want to try. Find a group that includes it. Whether it's a Facebook group, a Substack chat thread or something local, start showing up in places that reflect who you're becoming.

And if you're a writer or creative (or just someone with something to say), come join my Writers in the Wild community. It's for women who are ready to be seen and heard, to share their stories aloud and to take their next bold step toward being published. We meet bi-monthly face-to-face and monthly on Zoom, and it's a ridiculously inspiring, real and uplifting space. Come sit with us. No pretence, no grammar police, just fun and like-minded friends. You can find the link on my website: www.rachaellawrence.co.uk/writers-in-the-wild

Surround Yourself With Expanders

Another thing that massively magnified my confidence? Role models, mentors, expanders – women who were already doing the things I wanted to do. There are so many women stepping up in the world right now, boldly showcasing their talents. There will be someone you connect with, whose content hits your soul, whose courage rubs off on you. Find them. Follow them. And for the love of all things good, tell them how they inspire you. DM them. Email them. Comment on their work.

The world needs more women cheering each other on instead of competing in silence.

I can tell you from personal experience, when a woman reaches out to me and says, "That podcast episode changed the way I see myself" or "That quote you posted three years ago? It still lives on my mirror," it means everything. It reminds me why I do what I do and affirms that I'm walking my talk.

Don't Be Afraid to Detox

Let's be honest. Some days, even the best affirmations and most inspiring content just don't land. When that happens, don't be afraid to step away. I'm a big fan of a digital detox, even if it's just a mini one. Put your phone down for a few hours. Check emails only once or twice a day. Choose a time block for social media and stick to it like your confidence depends on it, because it kind of does.

When you limit what you're absorbing, especially when you're feeling vulnerable, you create space to reduce your anxiety and hear your own voice again.

Curate a Space That Represents Who You're Becoming

My personal favourite way to reconnect with my power? Create a physical space that reflects who I'm stepping into.

And no, it doesn't have to be anything grand. Maybe you declutter your desk and light your favourite candle. Maybe you wrap your podcast mic in glitter vinyl (guilty) or paint your office corner pink with leopard print wallpaper (also guilty). You'd be surprised what a fresh bunch of flowers and a clear-out of your inbox can do for your soul. These little acts breathe new energy into your day and give you a sense of control when everything else feels a bit mad.

This space becomes your anchor, your creative corner, your reminder of where you're headed.

Build Your Personal Board of Directors

As you start to show up more powerfully and live in alignment with this bolder version of you, it's absolutely essential to surround yourself with people who see you, *really* see you and cheer you on.

Your energy is precious. So let's be intentional about where it goes.

Create your own Board of Directors, your inner circle of people who remind you of your magic on the days you forget or when imposter syndrome tries to red light you. These are the women who clap for you when you're not in the room. The friends who lovingly call you out when you're in your own way. The mentors who reflect your potential back to you. The ones who will drag you out of the pit when you're about to quit on yourself, hand you a coffee and say, "Nope. You're not done yet."

Take a good, hard look at your current circle.

Who inspires you?

___

Who drains the hell out of you?

___

Who motivates you to rise?

___

Start there.

Then nurture the relationships that energise you and gently create space from the ones that don't. And if you're struggling to find your crew, hire a coach or join a community that aligns with your next level. Because you're not meant to do this alone. And you don't have to.

Final Thoughts

You didn't come this far to hand your power back to old habits or outdated opinions. You've peeled back the layers, stared down your fears and realigned with your truth and that deserves to be protected fiercely.

Staying in your power isn't about never wobbling. It's about knowing how to recalibrate quickly. It's about choosing you, again and again, even when the external noise gets loud and the familiar patterns start whispering your name.

This chapter isn't about becoming someone new; it's about standing firm in who you already are. You've done the inner work, faced the discomfort and made choices that align with the woman you're becoming.

Now it's about protecting that growth with the same energy you used to create it. You're not responsible for other people's reactions to your evolution, and you're certainly not here to make everyone comfortable. You are here to grow, to evolve and take up space that was always meant for you.

So when life tests you (because it will), and when the critics, the doubters and even your inner bitch voice try to pull you back, you'll stand taller. You'll remember who the hell you are. And you'll keep going. You've come too far not to.

What matters now is that you trust your own voice, honour your boundaries and stay focused on what truly matters to you.

On the days when doubt creeps in or the noise gets loud, return to your truth. Keep choosing yourself, even when it's hard. Especially when it's hard. Your growth is valid. Your vision is clear.

Your power is not up for negotiation.

Confidence Cues

The real test of transformation is staying empowered when life and people try to pull you back into old roles.

- Not everyone will celebrate your glow-up. Shine anyway.

- You don't need everyone to get it; you need *you* to.

- Your power doesn't need permission to be present.

- Pushback is proof of growth. Keep going.

- Confidence means holding your ground, even when it shakes.

- Choose a board of directors that will call you forward, not drag you back.

This is the power era, darling. Own it.

"The most magnetic woman in the room is the one who refuses to apologise for existing."

Conclusion

If you've reached this point, congratulations! You've done the hard work to ditch imposter syndrome, silence your inner critic and step into your confidence.

Take a breath, love, pause and soak this moment in. You've come further than you realise.

Think about where you were when you opened this book. Maybe you were sat at the kitchen table, late at night, desperately reworking the slides for a work presentation, convinced your boss will finally see you're a fraud and fire you on the spot.

Maybe you were hovering over your phone, crafting and deleting emails asking for a raise, because deep down, you're sure they'll laugh you out of the office for even thinking you deserve more.

Or maybe, like so many of us, you were watching your friends, colleagues and strangers on Instagram celebrate career wins, book deals or successful business launches and thinking, "Why does this look so easy for everyone else? When will it finally feel easy for me?"

You might've even caught yourself dreaming of a day your fairy godmother appears, and with a glitter-covered magic wand, instantly restores your confidence and puts all the pieces back together for you.

But you and I both know, deep down, no fairy godmother is coming.

There's no quick fix, no perfect moment waiting around the corner to magically erase the overwhelm, the nagging doubts or the sinking fear of being found out.

This is the reality of imposter syndrome. It's real, it's exhausting and it shows up when you least expect it.

It rears its ugly head during family dinners when someone innocently asks what you do for a living, and you fumble your response, convinced you're boring them or sounding ridiculous. It creeps up at networking events where you awkwardly shuffle your feet, telling yourself you don't belong in a room full of accomplished women. It hits you right before you press publish on a vulnerable social media post, convinced the trolls will tear you apart and expose you as a fraud.

These moments, these real, raw scenarios, aren't just inconvenient. They're stealing your joy, your brilliance and your potential, one anxious, self-doubting thought at a time. And my love, we can't afford to let that happen anymore. It's time we rewrite this bullshit once and for all.

I've been you. I know exactly how it feels to be standing on the edge of your life, questioning your worth, doubting your potential and feeling trapped by invisible barriers. But here's the beautiful thing: by picking up this book, you chose to do something about it. And, more importantly:

You chose yourself.

In reading this book, you've done more than simply acknowledge your struggles; you've actively challenged them. You've begun to dismantle outdated beliefs, confronted perfectionism head-on and taken significant steps towards fully reclaiming your power and confidence. That in itself is remarkable.

But let me be crystal clear. This is not where this empowering journey ends; it's just the beginning.

What happens next is where the real magic unfolds. Because your transformation isn't something you get to tick off a checklist. It's a daily practice, a beautiful, sometimes and often, messy commitment to yourself.

It's choosing every single day to show up as the most authentic, courageous, unapologetic version of you. Even when it's uncomfortable, even when it scares you, even when you're not entirely sure what the fuck you're supposed to do next.

And now, my love, you're ready…

Because you understand that your value no longer depends on perfection, on other people's validation or external, societal measures of success. You know that the life you've secretly been craving is not only possible, it's waiting patiently for you to claim it.

This book was always more than just strategies for silencing your inner critic or ditching imposter syndrome. It was about finally giving yourself permission to say, "It's my time, it's my turn," to live your life exactly how you want to, on your own terms. It was about reclaiming your dreams and desires, putting yourself first for once and refusing to settle for anything less than the life that excites and fulfils you completely.

You're no longer available for living someone else's narrative. You no longer need permission to show up fully. You no longer allow other people's fears, expectations or judgements to hold you back.

You're now leading with *clarity, conviction and authenticity.*

Think about how it feels to embody this shift fully. Imagine walking into meetings without second-guessing your value, standing confidently in conversations where your opinion matters.

Imagine waking up each morning with purpose and excitement for your day, no longer dreading the obligations that previously weighed you down. Picture yourself building authentic relationships, both personal and professional, that uplift and energise you instead of drain you.

Because this is exactly what happens when you step fully into your power and refuse to dim your light for anyone.

I wrote this book from the messy trenches of my own lived experiences. I've walked every step of this journey alongside you. I've felt the crushing weight of imposter syndrome, been paralysed by perfectionism and navigated toxic friendships and challenging workplaces.

Through it all, I've learned one crucial truth: Your story is your strength.

Your unique experiences, your wisdom gained from setbacks and struggles – these are the foundation of your greatest power.

Turning your shit into gold isn't just something I made up after a few margaritas; it's a call to action. It's your blueprint for living boldly, bravely and brilliantly.

If I can reclaim my purpose, pivot courageously in midlife, build successful businesses, create meaningful relationships, marry again and show up as my truest self after decades of doubt, criticism and setbacks, then I know without a shadow of doubt that you can too.

I promise you your midlife isn't a fucking crisis. It is your awakening, your turning point, your brightest chapter yet.

If there's one final message I want to leave with you, it's this:

You are worthy of a life that feels like home.

You deserve to show up fully, confidently, every single day. You're not here to play small. You're here to create impact, show up authentically and feel joy, abundance and deep fulfilment.

Your *Confident As F*ck* moment has already happened, the moment you opened this book and decided to begin this work.

Your rise? Darling, your rise is unstoppable.

But remember, sustaining this transformation requires community and support. It's crucial you surround yourself with people who see your magic, celebrate your growth and genuinely want you to succeed.

Women who lift you up, who hold you accountable with love, who remind you who you are when you forget.

That's exactly what I'm here for, too.

I'd love nothing more than to continue this journey with you beyond these pages. Because I deeply believe in your potential and am fiercely committed to seeing you fully step into it.

So let's keep this connection alive.

As a reader of *Confident as F*ck,* you get exclusive access to my custom Confident as Fuck Coaching GPT – your bold, 24/7 mindset coach and mentor in your pocket.

It's my gift to help you take the pressure off, ditch imposter syndrome and keep building your magnetic personal brand long after you've finished these pages.

Use it whenever you need a pep talk, a reset or a reminder that you are capable of so much more than you think. Consider it your private confidence hotline, available to readers of this book.

Confident As Fuck Coaching GPT

This totally free Coaching GPT (if you use ChatGPT) is available here: bit.ly/4oUMEof.

Make sure you don't miss out! You can also scan this QR Code to get access:

Confident As Fuck 24/7 Coaching With Rachael

SCAN ME

I have also made all the resources and activities in this book available for free on my website. Get the best guidance and templates for The Confidence Power Practice, Main Character Affirmations and the Money & Worth Alignment Wheel in the Book Bonuses page online.

Book Bonuses

SCAN ME

Download your bonuses here: https://rachaellawrence.co.uk/book-bonuses. Use the password BOOKBONUSES.

The first book I wrote, the one that changed it all for me, is also available on Amazon or at bit.ly/42UTpxI. Come join me and *Reset Your Mind.*

Your dreams don't stop here. Your growth doesn't have an expiry date. This is simply your starting point, your foundation for the beautiful, abundant life you're building every day from here on out.

Today, I invite you to celebrate how far you've already come. Celebrate your wins, big and small. Celebrate your courage. Celebrate the incredible, brave, wise woman staring back at you in the mirror.

And above all, celebrate your willingness to be as confident as fuck, reclaim your worth and rise into your fullest potential. In doing so, you're creating a ripple effect; your courage empowers the women around you to rise alongside you. And that, my love, is exactly how we do life now.

You're not alone anymore.
Your dreams matter. Your voice matters. You matter.
And from this moment on, you are unstoppable.

Now go out into the world and show them exactly who the fuck you are.

With love, fierce belief and absolute admiration,

Rachael xoxo
(Your forever biggest fan)

References

Chapter 1

[1] KPMG, *Advancing the Future of Women in Business: A KPMG Women's Leadership Study*, New York, KPMG LLP, 2020.

[2] Shaw, J., *The Confidence Trap: How Perfectionism Sabotages Success*, New York, HarperCollins, 2020.

[3] Huecker, M., *Imposter Syndrome and Burnout: How Perfectionism Keeps Women Stuck*, London, Women's Health Press, 2023.

[4] Peng, H., Teplitskiy, M., Romero, D. M. and Horvát, E.-A., 'Gender Differences in Self-Promotion: Evidence from a Field Experiment', *Nature Human Behaviour*, vol. 9, no. 2, 2025.

[5] NationalWorld, 'Women Begin to Feel Invisible by Age 36, Survey Finds', *NationalWorld*, London, NationalWorld Publishing, 2025, https://www.nationalworld.com (accessed 10 October 2025).

Chapter 2

[6] Weight Watchers UK, 'Women Criticise Themselves Eight Times a Day, Study Reveals', *Weight Watchers UK*, London, Weight Watchers UK, 2016, https://www.weightwatchers.com/uk (accessed 10 October 2025).

Chapter 3

[7] Lally, P., van Jaarsveld, C. H., Potts, H. W. and Wardle, J., 'How Are Habits Formed: Modelling Habit Formation in the Real World', *European Journal of Social Psychology*, vol. 40, no. 6, 2009, pp. 998–1009.

Chapter 7

[8] HRD Connect, 'Almost Half of Women in the UK Feel Underpaid', *HRD Connect*, London, HRD Publishing, 2024, https://www.hrdconnect.com (accessed 10 October 2025).

Printed in Dunstable, United Kingdom

78183708R00127